Tiln & Other Plays

Michael Cook
Tiln & Other Plays

published with assistance from the Canada Council

Talonbooks
201 1019 East Cordova
Vancouver
British Columbia V6A 1M8
Canada

This book was typeset by Gretchen Amussen at B.C. Monthly Typesetting Service, designed by David Robinson and printed by Hemlock Printers for Talonbooks.

First printing: December 1976.

Talonplays are edited by Peter Hay.

"Tiln" was first published in *Encounter: Canadian Drama in Four Media*, Eugene Bensen, ed., Toronto, Methuen, 1973.

"Therese's Creed" was commissioned by Centaur Theatre, Montréal, Québec.

Rights to produce "Tiln," "Quiller" or "Therese's Creed" from *Tiln & Other Plays*, in whole or in part, in any medium by any group, amateur or professional, are retained by the author and interested persons are requested to write to him at P.O. Box 327, R.R. #1, Petley, Random Island, Trinity Bay, Newfoundland A0E 1J0.

Canadian Cataloguing in Publication Data

Cook, Michael, 1933—
    Tiln & other plays

    Contents: Tiln. — Quiller. —
Therese's creed.
    ISBN 0-88922-107-3 pa.

    I. Title. II. Title: Quiller.
III. Title: Therese's creed.
PS8555   C812'.5'4   C77-002030-5
PR9199.3

Tiln was first produced by CBC Radio Studio 71 on August 29, 1971, with the following cast:

Tiln	Hugh Webster
Fern	Joe Austin

Produced by Jean Bartels

Quiller was first performed at Memorial University, St. John's, Newfoundland, in April, 1975, with the following cast:

Quiller	Clyde Rose

Directed by Al Pittman

Quiller was also performed by Giant's Head Theatre in Summerland, B.C., with the following cast:

Quiller	David Ross

Directed by Ken Smedley

Tiln

TILN is of indeterminate age, powerful, pos-
sessed at times of a near demonic vocal energy,
at once desolate, triumphant, gentle, arrogant. . .
A man living on the exposed edge of his soul.

FERN is frail, weak. His appearance suggests
that he is sixty-five or seventy.

The setting of the play is the interior of a lighthouse. This lighthouse must contain the illusion
that it is a platform on the edge of space and
time. This effect may be obtained by the use of
an arc light suspended directly over the playing
area, the edges trimmed to give the illusion of an
expanding cylindrical shape.

At the centre of the lighthouse is a winding
tubular steel staircase leading up to the light
platform which is a low railed circular steel
plate. A binnacle light occupies most of this
space. As they are now difficult to obtain,
it is only necessary to have a skeleton outline
of the light, but it must rotate on its axis, be

able to be locked into position, and be hinged on one side with a glass window. It is necessary that the lamp is seen because it is to be lit. There should be just sufficient space around the lamp for TILN to move about the platform. Given the concept of light creating the illusion of the structure, the dressing and properties are only those with a specific function within the context of the text.

Leaning against the rail, there is a double-barrelled, twin-hammered shotgun, the type common in the late 19th Century. There should be a small ledge on which rests a tinder box used for lighting the oil-fired lamp.

Below the platform, there is a wooden frame cot which is FERN's bed. There is an ancient horn gramaphone, preferably with a bamboo needle, and a 78 recording of "Eternal Father Strong to Save." Conceivably, copies of this 78 may be in short supply, and they certainly would suffer from being destroyed nightly during the course of the play. However, it would be nice if the breaking of the record could be done authentically, but it is not essential. There is also a large barrel able to accommodate FERN; a sack of salt; a Bible, which is kept by FERN in his cot; an early 19th Century chest with brass locks and a small, three-legged stool.

The stage is in darkness. The sound of wind and sea and the screeching of gulls is heard. The sounds fade, but not completely. Still in darkness, TILN begins his slow ascent up the iron staircase. He takes three steps. His boots ring on the metal staircase. The lights come up slowly. They reveal him standing on the third step. He is dressed simply in a fisherman's sweater and wears dark baggy trousers, which are tucked into the tops of a pair of heavy grey socks which

*emerge just above his seaman's boots. He looks
out and down and begins by counting the steps
he has taken.*

TILN:

Three.

> *He listens to the sound of the sea and the wind.
> He continues to climb slowly, heavily, taking
> three more steps. The sounds fade.*

And three. Six. Why am I proceeding in odd numbers?
Only to arrive at even numbers?

> *He moves up six more steps, counting to him-
> self. He pauses.*

Twelve.

> *There is one more step to get up onto the plat-
> form. The wind and sea sounds erupt, then fade.*

Shall I do the last? Will it be the last time that I do
the last? That any of us do?

> *He pauses and chuckles, pauses again and frowns.*

Each time is the last time. Something dies.

> *A gull screeches. The sound is deafening, rau-
> cous — greedy.*

Scream on, scream on. I've all the wings and waves
and words at my disposal. I'll take my time.

> *The gull screams again, as if in reply. There is
> a call made by sea gulls which sounds like a
> rather mocking terrier-like yap. This call should
> be inserted here. TILN shouts.*

Be off or I'll take the gun to ye.

He listens, as if for a reply. There is only the sound of the sea and the wind.

Ach. I shouldn't have said that. It's not right after all. One of God's numerous dumb creatures. It's not as if it's human.

He pauses, surprised.

Mmph. That's what Fern would say.

He pauses.

Fern.

The gull screeches again. TILN shouts.

It's not as if you're human.

The sound of the sea and the wind is heard.

Well, a step more, a step less. It's of no matter.

He takes the last step to get up onto the platform.

There.

He moves around the rim, looking out over the rails. There is an upsurge of wind, a roaring of the waves. It fades down.

What a world! What a table of . . .

He pauses.

Spread with . . . Laid on . . . The cold handkerchief of the Lord. Rock and waste. Desolation and water.

The gulls scream derisively.

All the colours of the world. All the colour left in the world. Black. White. Dark green. The colour of doom.

He laughs.

Dark green. We all turn. Happens to us all.

He pauses and looks out.

It's beautiful. Holy.

The sea and wind sounds rise rhythmically, steadily. TILN chants above it, raising his arms.

In the beginning was the water . . . Gospel according to Saint Tiln. Then storm. Then cloud. Then the splitting. Then the upheaving. The boiling rock cascading. Then God. And after . . . Tiln.

The sea and wind sounds fade.

ME. Tiln.

He lowers his arms and looks about, as if expecting to see someone, as if he has been overheard. He then chuckles, hugs himself and laughs outloud.

Just a crazy old man spilling his brains to the wind.

The gull screeches again. He suddenly rages.

What. You'd mock Tiln, would you? I'll show you.

He reaches for the shotgun, turns and fires both barrels out over the audience. The screeching dies abruptly. He leans on the gun.

Can't even get civility from gulls anymore. Once when I was younger . . .

He pauses.

If a man can't get civility from gulls anymore . . .
If a man can't keep his environment in order, he's
doomed. Doomed.

> *He replaces the shotgun and pauses. He makes a
> decision.*

It's time for the weather.

> *He paces about the platform, looking out.*

Yes. Getting dark. Yes. Wind backing westerly.
Cumulus, angels of the storm, piling up in the north-
west. Yes . . . Yes . . . Yes.

> *Getting excited.*

The sea running like a stallion about to break from
the pen. Good. The question is . . . as it always is.
Shall I light the lamp? If I light it, we may not be
disturbed. And then again, if I don't light it . . .

> *He pauses.*

If I don't light it, it is possible, improbable, but just
possible, that a few potential disturbers won't rumple
their foolish beds ever again. Won't ever turn in the
warm dark to the dark warm flesh . . . Be instead
a fishy hermaphrodite to the nuzzling cod.

> *He pauses.*

It's a difficult choice. Very difficult.

FERN: *weakly*
       Tiln.

We have not been aware of FERN until this moment. He has been lying on his cot, covered with a blanket. Now he raises himself weakly and calls again up the staircase.

Tiln.

The voice is a voice of intrusion. TILN stares out over the waves. The sound rises and falls.

Tiln.

TILN: *annoyed, shouting*
What is it?

FERN:
What were you firing at, Tiln?

TILN:
A gull. Only a gull.

To himself.

Old fool.

FERN:
Again, Tiln?

There is a pause. The sound rises and falls.

They're all God's creatures, Tiln. God's creatures.

Another pause. The sound rises and falls again. FERN listens intently.

Tiln? Are you there?

TILN: *roaring*
Of course, I'm here. Where else would I be? Where else is there?

There is a pause.

FERN:
Have you lit the lamp, Tiln?

Another pause. The sound rises and falls.

Have you lit the lamp?

TILN: *savagely*
There's none left to light the lamp for.

FERN:
They're all God's creatures, Tiln.

TILN:
There's none worth lighting the lamp for.

He pauses.

No one ever lit the lamp for me. I survived. Tiln survived.

He pauses.

I said . . . Tiln survived.

FERN:
One of God's creatures.

He pauses.

Light the lamp, Tiln.

TILN: *to himself*
Light the lamp, light the lamp. Old and broken, he lies there, like a worn out shoe. Light the lamp. He's dying. It'll be mine when he's dead. The lighthouse will be all mine when he's dead. As it used to be.

He pauses and shouts down to FERN.

If God had meant lamps to be lit, he'd have hung them in the Garden of Eden.

FERN does not answer. He stays sitting up, listening intently. There is a sudden cacophony of gulls. TILN says with disgust . . .

Yes, yes. You may be right. The world belongs to the white winged scavenger defecating across continents.

He moves rapidly to the shotgun, breaks it, and fumbles in his pocket for shells. He re-loads.

Oh, you are beautiful. You're ecstatic. Gliding on the currents of air that ruffle the heads of the waves. A marvel of nature.

He suddenly aims and fires, backstage.

There. And there. You may shit on my kingdom, but I am still God. Tiln . . . God of the wilderness.

He peers out and down.

Your blood glows, spotting the white and green slaver of the seas. In death, you are beautiful, magnificent. Not like us. Not like us at all. But I am Tiln come to his inheritance. A rock. A light that I may not light.

There is an upsurge in sound of gulls screeching.

More. And yet more.

With savagery.

Then I will light candles for you.

He opens the lamps, takes the tinder, lights the lamp, and slams the lamp door shut. He spins the lamp around.

I will light you a path across the waves. Do I dazzle you?

He suddenly stops the spinning lamp and locks it into position.

There.

He laughs.

Now it is a great unblinking eye that never moves. Why should it illuminate more than one corner of the wasted universe? Enough is enough.

The screeching of gulls is heard.

Yes. Fly. Fly. Trapped in the light. The great unseeing eye that blinds. Fly on . . . Yes, that's it, out of the blackness, flying blind. I am Lord of the universe still.

FERN:
Tiln. Have you lit the lamp?

TILN laughs.

TILN:
Yes. Yes, Fern. I have lit the lamp.

FERN:
Is it turning smoothly on its axis?

TILN:
It is on its axis.

He laughs.

Fern?

FERN:

Yes.

TILN:

I am coming now.

> *He checks about him, then moves a step off the platform.*

All blind now. Black. Except for the cyclops. One unseeing unmoveable eye.

> *He moves down three steps and pauses.*

The only eye.

> *He moves down three more steps.*

Pitiless.

> *He moves down three more steps.*

As malevolent as the bitch that raised me.

> *He pauses, three steps from the bottom. FERN, with great difficulty, shuffles from his cot towards the gramaphone. He winds it painfully.*

I can't see.

> *Agonized.*

I can't see.

> *He shuffles back to his cot. The record is the hymn "Eternal Father Strong to Save, Whose Arm Doth Bind the Restless Wave." He sits up on his cot. Tears stream down his face. TILN*

remains rooted three steps up. FERN occasional-
ly mumbles with the last word of a line. The
first verse ends.

TILN:

    God.

    He shouts it.

God.

    The next verse begins. TILN, after a pause,
    comes rapidly down into the room.

Fern. I am here. Tiln . . . is here.

    FERN feebly hums with the hymn.

Up there, Fern, up there . . . is the dying wave.

    The hymn plays on. FERN looks at TILN.

FERN:

    You have lit the lamp?

TILN:

    Yes.

    FERN hums.

FERN:

    I am dying, Tiln.

TILN:

    So are we all.

FERN:

    But not immediately.

TILN:

    Immediately.

FERN:

You should not rage so.

TILN:

Rage!

He moves quickly to the gramaphone. He tears the needle across the remainder of the record. The sound wails and dies. He crosses to FERN.

I, Tiln, looked out across my world. It was all in order. The confusion of the waves. I felt a promise of thunder. Saw the gulls, hunchbacked, folded for the fall. I felt as if . . .

FERN:

Yes.

TILN:

Wind. The wave. Rock. No one. Everything absolute. The stock polished and smooth in my hands.

FERN:

Yes.

TILN:

The shells in the breech.

FERN:

Yes.

TILN:

Everything mine. Nobody there.

FERN:

Yes.

TILN:

The stock in my hand . . . The rock . . . Myself growing from the rock. Like some desolate anemone.

FERN:
> Yes.

TILN:
> As it has always been.
>
> *Struggling.*
>
> Why did you call me?
>
> *He pauses.*

FERN:
> I am dying, Tiln.
>
> *There is a pause.*

TILN:
> I know.

FERN:
> Tiln. The ice is coming.

TILN: *exulting*
> Borne on the Labrador Current. Yes. The ice is coming. Shapes of my childhood in the sand, overriding, cracking.

FERN:
> What will you do with me?

TILN: *surprised*
> When?

FERN:
> When I am dead?

TILN:
> I have thought about it.

FERN:
> There will be no relief.

TILN:
> No.

FERN:
> Ever?

TILN:
> No.

FERN:
> It's not that I mind the sea bed.

TILN:
> No.

FERN:
> I have seen it when the sea recedes.

TILN:
> The sea bed?

FERN:
> Yes.

TILN:
> But the ice.

FERN:
> Yes.

> *He pauses.*

> How will you?

> *There is a pause.*

> It is not as if it were spring.

TILN:

I have thought about it. Often. The barrel. The brine. The head erect on its pillar of salt.

He pauses.

FERN:

Ah.

He pauses.

I would like a service, Tiln.

TILN:

I do not believe in service.

FERN: *anguished*
I have been good to you.

TILN:

We have been good to each other.

FERN:

We have kept the light.

TILN:

I do not believe in light.

FERN:

But you . . . You were the one who lit it.

TILN:

It was not my light.

He pauses.

It was never my light. It was your light. I had lived happily with its blind eye. Cyclops.

He pauses.

FERN:

But you lit it.

TILN:

Because you cried out of the darkness.

There is a pause.

FERN:

Yes. We have been good to each other. Ten years . .

TILN:

Each other's hands . . .

FERN:

Eyes.

He pauses.

Each other's minds.

TILN:

Fog and ice.

FERN:

Storm and tidal wave.

TILN:

Grapnel and rope.

FERN:

Flare and winch.

TILN:

It was . . .

FERN:

Yes.

TILN:

It was the work of a medieval priest.

FERN:

> Without a parish.

> *He pauses.*

> I need a service, Tiln.

TILN:

> I do not believe in service.

FERN:

> Then I shall be unable to die.

> *He pauses.*

> I will not go without a service.

> *He pauses, passionate and breathless.*

> I will not spend eternity crying on the wind. You
> have heard them, Tiln? Tiln . . . You have seen them,
> hunted by gulls in the mist, fishy phantoms for every
> bird of prey.

> *He pauses.*

> Tiln. You have watched them at the helm of dead
> ships steering past the eye of the light hard onto the
> rocks.

> *He pauses.*

> Tiln. You have cowered at their carousing . . . At the
> oaths flickering like lightning in the maelstrom of
> the hurricane, in the breath of hot air that lurks, an
> obscenity, on the heel of the northeast wind.

> *There is a pause. FERN searches TILN's face for
> an answer. TILN is implacable.*

> You would make me one with them.

TILN:

    I would be God.

       He pauses.

    You have told me . . . often. There might be others.

       He is avoiding the issue.

    You said once . . .

       FERN is desperate. He hunts amongst the blankents and finds the Bible. He opens it.

FERN:

    See . . . I had left it . . . It is there. A few words, that is all.

       He holds it out to TILN, who ignores it.

    The book is open. The words are marked . . .

TILN:

    When will you die?

FERN:

    I don't know. Soon.

TILN:

    How soon?

FERN:

    I don't know. I need a service.

TILN:

    I don't believe in service.

FERN: *crying out*
    I don't know what to do.

       TILN laughs.

FERN:

God, God. What should I do?

TILN:

Celebrate the magnificence of life.

He takes the Bible from FERN and begins to read.

"Lord. Thou has been our refuge from one generation to another . . ."

FERN:

We have been brothers, Tiln.

TILN:

"Before the mountains were brought forth or ever the earth and the world were made . . ." I like that. It has a nice ring to it. But we are on the rock. Which is on the earth. Which is the world. It's not good enough.

FERN:

We were not insignificant, Tiln.

He pauses.

Tiln?

TILN: *reading*

"Thou carriest them away as with a flood and they are even as a sleep. In the morning they are like grass that groweth up."

FERN:

We were of service, Tiln. We were of service.

TILN: *reading*

"For when thou art angry all our days are gone. We bring our years to an end, as it were a tale that is told . . ."

FERN:
Tiln. Tiln . . . the service . . .

TILN: *enraged*
By an idiot. An idiot.

He hurls the Bible across the room.

There's your service for you. Service. Light. Signifi-
cant. Insignificant. Is it of any consequence, Fern?
Does it matter that you are dying? That the light is
fixed? Immoveable?

Suddenly, he howls.

Oh, where are the cities of my childhood? The
streets . . . thronging. The faces . . . the faces . . .

FERN: *in pain*
I am dying, Tiln.

TILN:
The dying faces.

*FERN struggles to get off his cot. He stands,
totters, nearly falls and begins to shuffle towards
TILN. TILN backs away.*

Get away from me. Dead man. Get away.

FERN: *in a whisper*
The service. The service, Tiln.

*He shuffles after him. TILN crosses him to the
edge of the light.*

TILN:
Can't you even die alone. That's not much to ask.

*FERN sees the Bible. He shuffles towards it and
picks it up.*

27

FERN:

Out of the depths have I cried to thee, O Lord. Lord, hear my voice . . . Oh, let thine ears consider well the voice of my complaint.

TILN:

Stop it, Fern.

Threatening him.

Stop it. That service is not enough. It is a dead service.

FERN: *whispering*
If Thou, O Lord, will be extreme to mark what is done amiss. O Lord, who may abide it . . .

TILN:

Fern, I, Tiln, will provide the service.

FERN: *pausing*
Yes. We have been good to one another.

He is breathing with difficulty. He reads again from the Bible.

Let thine ears consider well the voice of my complaint.

TILN:

Fern. Enough.

FERN:

Out of the depths . . .

TILN strides across to him and knocks the Bible from his hand. He shakes him like a dog.

TILN:

Enough, I say.

He picks him up beneath with one arm and carries him across to his cot. He throws him down on it like a rag doll.

Like a gull, screeching. Above. Below. Ach. Do you hear me, Fern, you're like a gull? You will end like a gull. Salted down, blown wide. I'm sick of your "Have you lit the lamp, Tiln?"

He mimics.

"I am dying, Tiln." Let me examine you. Mmph. As I thought. You are the living dead. Eyes . . . opaque, filmed. Skin, coarse, bad smelling. Bristles like a porcupine. Scar.

He pauses. He touches it gingerly with one finger and jumps back.

The burn. It is livid, Fern. Glowing.

He breaks from him and strides about the room agitatedly.

Tale told by an idiot. Always your tales. The bomb. The mangled children. God's face in the sky. Never my tales. Not Tiln's emptiness. No voiding for Tiln.

He pauses.

Who was it saved you? Who was it dragged you from your boat more dead than alive? As now. I . . . I, Tiln.

FERN: *very faintly, a death rattle in his throat*
Tiln . . .

With energy and purpose, TILN drags a barrel to the centre.

TILN:
>There. I've always known it would come to this. Here's your coffin, Fern. Mmmm. Nice workmanship. Tapers smoothly at each end. The hoops are firm.

>*He tests them then crosses to FERN.*

>Tiln giveth. Tiln taketh away. That's your service. Up you come.

>*He picks FERN up like a sack of straw.*

FERN: *very faintly*
>We have been good to each other.

TILN:
>I've got it all ready. It's always been ready. I knew it would come to this. There . . .

>*He drops FERN into the barrel. FERN's head flops grotesquely over the rim.*

>Don't flop about so. Where's your dignity? Salt. Salt . . .

>*He fetches a sack of salt and opens it.*

FERN:
>Tiln . . .

>*He gasps.*

TILN: *pouring the salt into the barrel*
>There's brine for you. There's a lifetime of tears.

>*FERN gasps. TILN empties the sack and turns and fetches another. There must be enough salt to fill the barrel up to FERN's shoulders. TILN continues panting.*

>There. That should do it. Are you comfortable?

FERN gasps unintelligibly.

And now it's my turn. It is time for my story.

He pauses.

No more interruptions. No ulcerated conscience. No bleating sheep.

He sings, "Eternal Father Strong to Save." He gets up, fetches the three-legged stool and brings it back tothe barrel. He sits down in front of FERN and looks at him. He scratches his head, gets up and walks around the room. He laughs to himself and scratches his head.

Humph. I feel . . . Hhhhmp. Enlivened. No. That's not it. Weightless then? As of one suddenly freed from the ordure of the earth. Hmmph.

He crosses back and sits in front of FERN.

I . . .

He pauses, puzzled.

I don't know what to say. After all this time. Planning. Lapsing at times into visions.

He peers closely at FERN and shakes his head. His head lolls from one side of the barrel to the other.

Fern?

He shouts in FERN's ear.

Fern? Pay attention. Focus on the light.

He sits back on the stool.

To begin in the beginning. Once upon a time, I was fishing.

He pauses. He cocks his head forward to FERN's mouth, to see if he is breathing.

Are you listening, Fern?

FERN gasps weakly.

Good. I was fishing.

He pauses.

Oh, how the sun sparkled on the water. I remember looking up at the sky. At the wheeling gulls. There wasn't another boat for miles.

He pauses.

There wasn't another boat. It was all emptiness. It was all creation. It was mine. The water. The sunlight on the water. The gulls. The corks bobbing in the sun. The trap baited. I remember . . .

A pause.

I remember looking up at the sky. Fern? You're not listening. Remember . . . I have the gun, Fern . . . The gun . . .

He gets up rapidly, swings towards the stairs and mounts it with speed and agility. He pauses briefly at the top, delighted with himself.

Freed from the ordure of the earth.

He picks up the shotgun and is about to descend, but he pauses once again.

The weight of the world's whey.

He rushes down the stairs and pauses at the foot.
He fumbles for shells, breaks and loads the
shotgun, and crosses to FERN, cocking his head
to hear if FERN is still breathing.

You were not listening, Fern.

He raises the shotgun and fires one barrel,
inches away from FERN's ear. FERN does not
move. TILN sits.

Pay attention, I warn you.

Petulant.

You won't be able to say I didn't warn you.

He pauses.

Where was I?

He pauses and thinks.

Ah, yes. I remember looking up at the sky. That's
it. In my head, a film unrolling. Journeying. Travel-
ling. People half remembered. Voice on the wind.
Fragments of conversation. Women I had loved remembered now not for their bodies but for an im-
pression of warmth. Mmmph. Odd that. An impres-
sion of warmth.

He pauses.

Looking up . . . Remembering . . . Thinking how all
had changed. How I had not seemed to change.

He pauses.

Looking up at the sky . . . At the clattering gulls.

Suddenly angry.

Gulls. If a man can't control his environment . . .
Where was I? . . .

FERN: *gasping, but suddenly clear*
Tiln. We have . . . We have.

TILN: *leaning forward and putting his arm round FERN's
shoulders, which are just visible* And you came then,
Fern. Drifting up out of the south. Your arm trailing
in the bright water as a bird's wing trails across low
cloud. I remember thinking. . . An odd way to fish . . .

He pauses, laughs, and withdraws his arm.

Yes. An odd way to fish. And then I remember
thinking, I have the gun. Yes. I have the gun. I felt
it then. The stock oiled and polished. Slipping easily
in my hands.

He pauses.

There was something about the manner of your
coming that . . . Something . . . Fern.

He pauses.

Fern. I have not told you this. There was something
about the manner of your coming that disturbed me.
You were, after all, coming from the direction I had
not left, but one in which I refused to go. Yes.

He pauses.

I remember . . .

With difficulty . . . Close to tears.

I remember. The first gull. It swooped low over your boat and settled on the stern . . . Looking at you.

He pauses.

I took no notice at first . . . Why should I? A boat. An arm trailing in the water. A gull watching as I watched.

He pauses.

But then came another. And another. And even again, another.

He pauses.

It was then that I thought you were dead.

He pauses, then starts excitedly:

The first one made a move towards your eyes. But I had the gun. As now. The stock fitted into my shoulder, smoothly. There was hardly a movement on the water. The sun spread out before me, power-fully, across the waves. The gun like a mast. Straight and steady, I fired.

He pauses.

Blood and feathers on the wave.

Angrily.

Gulls.

He pauses.

You stirred. Your boat then nudging mine, as a mongrel nudges the heel of his master.

He pauses.

Come to my mansion, I cried.

He pauses.

There is room.

He pauses.

There is light.

He pauses.

I remember looking up at the sky . . . It dazzled.

He pauses.

It rained light.

He pauses.

It rained leaves.

He pauses.

And then blood. The drops were warm. They stained my hands.

He pauses.

I had chosen not to go south. But it came to me, Fern.

Broken.

It came to me. Fern . . . Are you listening? Oh, you may gaze as sadly as you like from your dull eyes and your barrel of brine but you . . . You brought it with you, Fern. You brought it with you. A savaged prayer book. A gramaphone. A record.

In a swift, savage movement, he rises. He crosses to the gramaphone, picks up the record from the turntable, and breaks it over his knee. He grinds the pieces beneath his boots. There is a faint sound from FERN, as if something light and fragile and terribly lost had smattered itself against the leaded panes of the sky. TILN strides back to him.

Memories of . . . Thoughts of conscience. Your eyes were open when I carried you up the wet rock, your boat cast off, already drifting out to sea.

He pauses.

Your eyes were wide as I opened the door and you observed the roundness, the wholeness, the spiral steps leading up. To the light.

He pauses, then paces agitatedly.

Do you remember? . . .

He pauses.

Fern. Do you know? . . . Are you mindful of the first words that you uttered? Not a syllable on deliverance. No love. Not that one needs . . .

He pauses. Mimicking FERN, he says . . .

"It is getting dark. Go up and light the light."

He pauses. Speaking painfully.

Fern. You destroyed my . . .

He pauses. The sound of a storm building is heard. It commences quietly and increases in intensity from now to the end of play.

You took my . . .

He pauses. The storm is heard.

I believed that I did not need to know.

Through the storm, the screeching of gulls is heard.

Gulls!

He bends down over FERN.

I must leave you, Fern. I have to attend to the gulls. If a man can't control his environment . . .

Taking the shotgun, he begins to ascend the stairs. Slowly, as at the opening, he pauses after the third step.

Strange . . .

Slowly, he proceeds up three more steps.

I am shackled once more.

He proceeds up six more steps.

It is not that I was released.

He pauses.

That would put a different light upon it.

He pauses.

The last. Shall I do the last? Bound by the refuse of the earth.

He climbs onto the platform. The storm reaches violent proportions. Through and above the storm, the gulls sound a paean of mocking fury. TILN speaks in an anguished voice.

Leave me alone. Alone. You mock God. I, Tiln . . .

The cry echoes back to him . . . "I, Tiln . . . I, Tiln." It joins with the wind and wave sounds and gulls' cries. He puts the shotgun down and leans wearily against the rail, a tired old man, a prophet without people.

Something seems to have died.

He pauses, then shouts.

Rage on. You have no principality, no power. I am weary of you.

He pauses. Broken, he speaks . . .

Where are the lights? Where are the faces?

The storm rages, then fades. There is a lull.

Fern. Fern. I didn't finish. I did not tell you. There is no light. There are no travellers. There are none to save or destroy. Fern . . .

Louder.

Fern . . .

The vigour begins to flow back in him as he renews the dialectic with his soul.

You plagued me with your Christian conscience. Ringing like an alarm clock. Brrrrrh brrrrrh. Ringing.

Without the ring, no reason for its existence. We all record the passage of time. Ring, ring. Plaguing the elements. Even the gulls.

He pauses. A gull sound is heard. The storm cries.

I would have let you drift had I known. Let the gulls peck out your eyes. I was lonely, happy, lonely.

He shouts.

Two of us in a burgeoning universe and you have to be a martyr.

He pauses.

Well, I'm not sorry. You failed. You are no martyr, but my sacrifice. Me. God Tiln. Lord of the Light-house. Lord of the wind and wave. Lord of the gulls. Lord of the tilting universe.

The gulls reply, mocking. TILN's voice echoes back.

Tilting universe . . . Tilting universe . . . Mock on.

He shouts.

Mock on. Tonight, I give life to you. Tender you the benison of the streaming dark, the sanctuary of the wave.

He pauses and listens as the gulls' cries fade and the storm subsides.

So be it.

He pauses, then moves to the head of the stairs and listens again.

Fern. Fern . . .

He pauses.

Hurry, Fern. I'm waiting for your call.

> *He moves back to the rail and looks out.*
> *He stretches out both his hands, his palms*
> *upturned.*

It has started to rain.

> *He pauses.*

How gentle it is. Seeking the sockets of the eyes. The
furrows.

> *He pauses.*

It must be God. Crying.

> *He pauses.*

Now I remember all the rain of my days. The touch
and the taste varying with the contours of the wind.

> *He pauses.*

Fern.

> *Lovingly.*

Fern.

> *Tenderly submitting.*

I will rotate the light upon its axis.

> *He moves to the lamp, unclamps it, and spins*
> *it.*

There. The ceremony is ended.

He calls.

I'm coming, Fern.

He takes one step off the platform.

How could I let the gulls peck out his eyes?

He takes three more steps, then pauses.

I, Tiln. God of light. Of the tilting universe.

He takes three more steps, then pauses again.

Lord of the bladderwrack and the black sea moss.

He takes three more steps.

Keeper of the pearled and fishy parables of the sea.
Master of sailing barns.

He laughs.

Executioner. Jonah's hangman.

*He comes down the last three steps and moves
towards FERN.*

Fern. I have done it, Fern. The light is rotating on
its axis.

*He pauses, looks closely at FERN, reels back,
and roars with pain.*

Dead.

A cry of ultimate desolation.

Dead.

He crosses to barrel and kneels, cradling FERN's head in his arms.

You've cheated me, Fern . . . You've cheated me . . .

The lights fade. Hold in the black for thirty seconds. We hear TILN sobbing, and above, we see the lights from the lamp gleam.

Quiller

*The play is set on the bridge of an outport
house. A shingled roof slopes down across it
at a forty-five degree angle. The dimensions are
angular, to give the effect, not too exaggerated,
of drawing us towards the centre where there is
a door. To the right of the door is a day bed.
To the left, two ropes hang down, but the swing
seat they once supported is not in evidence.
There are no windows at the ground level.
Above the shingled roof line, the front of the
house rises upward. There are two windows
symmetrically aligned right and left above the
door — the eyes to the nose of the house. There
are blinds on the windows, which are white.
They are drawn to three inches above the sill.*

*The total effect is of perfect balance, harmony.
There is, however, a surrealistic effect to this
perfection. The clapboard exterior is white,
even, immaculate. The windows are identical.
The day bed, with its curved headboard, matches
the remainder. The woodwork gleams. The blan-
kets are without wrinkles. It has the sombre and*

*unnatural look of a coffin's interior. The ropes
hanging right are brand new manila. One spurt
of colour enlivens the monotony; the door knob
is brass, as is the lock plate. They gleam and
flash in the light.*

*There is no curtain. The audience may walk
through the set if they wish and, where possible,
sit around and almost on top of it. The play
opens with the following sequence . . .*

*The sun rises slowly on the audience. The set
remains in darkness, as if behind a hill.*

A cock crows.

The sun reaches the house.

The cock crows again.

*The door opens slowly. It closes to reveal
QUILLER.*

*QUILLER comes out to inspect the day. He is in
his mid-sixties, but there is little in his movement to suggest age. He is a powerful, grizzled
man, dressed in button-fly long johns and
matching Stanfield's woollen vest. He wears a
shiny, peaked, flat fisherman's cap. He comes
forward to the rail of the bridge. He looks out,
sweeps the sun-dazed audience/horizon with his
eyes. He scratches himself, yawns and pauses.*

*The sun rises slowly upon the house, and fades
on the audience.*

The cock crows again.

He goes to the left of the bridge and stares out.

QUILLER:
Taverner's is up late this marnin'.

> *He scratches himself and yawns again. Suddenly,*
> *he breaks forcefully into a hymn.*

"Will your anchor hold in the sea of life . . ."

> *He pauses.*

They's at it agin, I suppose. Ye'd think they'd quit
after twelve borned and ten running.

> *He turns and moves back centre. He looks out*
> *as before.*

Nar boat nor wave on the water. Sea be lonely, I
'low.

> *He turns to go back through the door, but*
> *pauses, his hand on the knob.*

Dat's strange . . . I left 'n open.

> *He turns to face out.*

Didn't I leave 'n open?

> *He turns back again and shakes his head. He*
> *opens the door and takes two paces through it.*
> *He turns again and checks the door to make sure*
> *it won't close behind him. He nods, satisfied,*
> *and disappears into the interior. There is a sixty-*
> *second pause. He emerges with an enamel bowl*
> *which contains a bar of old yellow soap and a*
> *shaving brush. He also carries a towel over his*
> *arm and a cut-throat razor. The latter is peril-*
> *ously hooked on the front of his long johns.*
> *He balances the bowl on the broad ledge of the*
> *bridge rail and drapes the towel beside it. He*
> *places the brush and the soap on the other side.*

*He picks up the brush and pauses. He puts it
down and looks behind himself. The door is
still open. He nods and goes back and closes the
door. Returning to the rail, he picks up the
brush and soap and begins to lather his face
vigorously, punctuating his actions with lines
from the hymn.*

"Will your anchor hold in the storms of life,
When the clouds unfold their wings of strife,
When the strong tides lift . . ."

*Nothing can be seen except his eyes. He fumbles
for the razor. It gets hooked in the top of his
long johns. There is a pause. He withdraws the
blade from his pants and begins to scrape.*

Marnin', Lord.

He scrapes.

Dis is your servant, Quiller.

*He scrapes, pauses, and cocks his head for a
reply. He nods.*

Dat's right too, Lord. I 'lows, ye knew it wor me all
the time.

He scrapes, pauses.

Ye mustn't mind me, Lord. I'm gittin' a bit foolish.

*An engine starts, off. It's an outboard. It slips
into gear and the boat whines off into the distance. He looks out and nods approvingly.*

Dat's better. Sea didn't look right at all.

He scrapes, pauses.

Don't sound too right wid them damn things, but I suppose it must take what it gits these days and be thankful fer it.

He scrapes and has finished — enough for him. He wipes the blade on the towel and hooks the razor back into his long johns. He wipes the remaining lather from his face with the towel. He pauses halfway through the operation and looks up.

Ye don't mind, do ye, if I don't take the trouble wi' it I used to? It's too tormentin', Lord, and being as 'ow ye've got a beard . . .

He finishes wiping his face, folds the towel and drapes it over the rail.

There I goes agin. Bein' too familiar.

He picks up the bowl and empties the water over the rail. Holding the bowl in one hand and a towel in the other, he takes the towel and wipes out the bowl. He stops, puzzled.

I did it agin. Four days together now. Or is it five?

He puts the bowl and towel back on the rail and picks up his shaving brush which is still covered in lather.

Is dat a sign, Lord?

He cocks his head for a reply. He looks disappointed.

I t'ought ye might be wantin' me to grow a beard, fer to correspond wit' yer image.

He shakes his head, wipes the brush on the bottom of the towel and then, gathering up the

49

artifacts of ablution, goes back to the door. He puts down the bowl. He opens the door and stoops to pick up the gear. He disappears inside, leaving the door open. He is gone for sixty seconds. From inside comes . . .

"Will your anchor hold in the sea of life,
When the clouds unfold . . ."

He reappears, carrying a mug of tea and a biscuit. The door closes behind him. He pauses, looks at the door, shakes his head and continues to the right, to the day bed. He sits, dips his biscuit in his tea and munches.

I don't mind tellin' ye, Lord, they is times when I gits disturbed.

He dips his biscuit in his tea.

Ye takes today now. Dat damn dicky bird o' Walter's wakes me up at five-thirty. Now, I knows me clock's been stopped this eight year, ever since . . .

He pauses and struggles with a recollection, but dismisses it.

And I knows the colour of yer sky, Lord, so I knows what five-thirty looks like every day o' the year, bright marnin's, dark marnin's and them in between. Ain't no one kin fool me on that.

He fumbles with his long johns where the razor was. He produces a small bag tied to somewhere inside the garment. It is tied around the neck with a string. He opens it, selects a biscuit, retightens the string, and pushes the bag back inside the long johns.

Five-thirty. I checks to see if Sadie's eaten her supper. And 'tis the same everyday. She done eaten the bread and left her tay. And fer a woman as powerful fond of her tay as Sadie, dat's strange. And then there's me brush.

He pauses, struggles for words.

What I'm trying to say, Lord, is dat the days is strange, but they is the same. There don't seem to be any difference, but they is all wrong.

He dips his biscuit in his tea.

So they's the dicky bird, and dat's the same. And they's me brush and Sadie's tay.

He pauses.

I comes down the stairs each marnin' and lights the stove wid the splits I 'ad in the oven the night afore, put there for the purpose. When she's goin' good I puts the kettle on the stove and comes out to say good day to ye, Lord, and to check on the rest of the sinners who pay little enough attention to ye or the dicky bird. And dat's the same.

He dips his biscuit.

But it ain't quite. They's somethin' strange in that too. Onced was I weren't the only one who talked to ye? Everyone talked to ye at one time or another. And not just because they was dying neither.

He dips his biscuit. He pauses and goes to take the biscuit out, but it's gone soggy and fallen into the mug. He roots around with his finger for the remains and licks off what he can find.

Then I goes and gits me gear fer shavin' and brings it out here. And fer the past four days I forgits to wash me brush afore I t'rows out the water. Or is it five days?

He pauses.

Dat's strange.

He pauses.

But it's becoming the same.

He pauses.

I don't rightly understand it.

A door bangs, off. He looks up sharply. He puts down his mug. A shouting of indistinguishable words is heard. A door bangs again. He gets up.

They's Uncle Luke. He's on the road early.

He moves quickly to the front rail.

Marnin', Luke, b'y. How is ye?

He pauses for a reply. None appears to be forth-coming.

You's early abroad.

He waits for an answer.

No. I never knew ye had that trouble. How are ye gittin' down?

Waiting for an answer.

No. I 'lows, He don't seem to hear as well as He should. Leastways, not all the time. But I'd prefer Him deaf to that young Ivany in the car.

Waiting for an answer.

Have ye time fer a mug o' tay?

Waiting for an answer.

No. I 'lows not. P'raps on yer way back then.

Waiting for an answer.

Aye.

He looks around at the sky.

'Tis a weather breeder.

His head and eyes follow LUKE down the road at the left. A car starts, off, and a door bangs. The car revs up; the engine roars. With a squeal of brakes it accelerates and the sound fades away. He shakes his head sadly.

Always did have trouble wid 'is ears, that one. What he had of 'n anyways. Apricot ears we used to call 'n. I mind Skipper Willis when Luke were crewman on his schooner and 'e went to 'n to sign off. "What fer?" says Skipper Willis. "I'm goin' to better meself," says young Luke. He wor young then. "I'm goin' clerkin' in St. John's" "Clerkin', is it?" says Skipper Willis. "If God 'ad meant ye to be a clerk, he'd a given ye ears to stick a pencil behind. Give over that foolishness." An' Luke, being a mite sensitive, give up the idea.

He pauses and goes back to the day bed. He sees his mug, sits, picks up mug and drains it.

Now, dat's strange. Here he be, goin' fer a hearin'
aid at his age. And it's too late fer him to take up
clerkin' now, I 'lows. But them hearin' aids 'as got
hooks to catch on behind yer ears. An' he ain't got
no ears to speak of.

He pauses.

I prays ye haven't got apricot ears, Lord, though I
knows dat whatever we got ye got in some shape or
another or however else would ye git to understand
it all.

*He heaves off the day bed and drops to his
knees.*

Dear Lord, this is thy servant, Quiller Laite, borned
these sixty-five years and still alive and thankin' ye
fer it. I knows I bin complainin', but it's not so much
o' dat as wonderin' and p'raps it's because I's ferget-
ful of all the t'ings ye've done fer me, fer I kin hear
the dicky bird which is more than Luke an' his
apricot ears, which I'm sure, Lord, ye didn't mean fer
him 'cos he's as good a man as ever walked abroad.
So I t'anks ye fer the light and fer the dark and the
wood in me stove and the water what don't be carry-
in' what it should, but is still there, and fer Sadie who
ye lets come back every night fer to eat her supper,
even if she don't drink her tay. And now here's a
hymn I wrote fer ye last night, if ye'll take it from
yer humble and obedient servant.

Hear these prayers, O Mighty Lord.
I tries to t'ink when I'm abroad
And if be chance they fails to rise,
I knows dat ye'll not be surprised,
But hope dat ye'll make up instead
The proper t'ings I should have said.

*He remains rapt in silent prayer. **The power of
his concentration is impressive, stirring. A stone***

*rattles onto the bridge. QUILLER remains
intent. Another stone lands, then another.
QUILLER starts, gets to his feet and rushes to
the front rail, then the right rail, then the left.*

Ye young divils. If I catches ye, I'll torment ye.

Children's voices are heard off.

FIRST CHILD: *off*
    It wor Brian, Mr. Laite.

SECOND CHILD:
    No, it weren't. It wor Michael.

QUILLER:
    I'll tan yer arses. The both of ye.

    *He makes no move however off the bridge, as if
    he were held by a force stronger than himself.*

FIRST CHILD:
    Ye'll have to catch us first.

    *A Coke can lands at QUILLER's feet. He roars
    impotently.*

SECOND CHILD:
    Things goes better wit' Coke.

FIRST CHILD:
    I bet Mrs. Ivany don't need Coke.

SECOND CHILD:
    Shall we tell Mrs. Ivany to come up to ye, Mr. Laite?

FIRST CHILD:
    No, b'y. What'd she want wid an old man like him?

SECOND CHILD:
    He's always shouting after her.

FIRST CHILD:

    I seen her onced. Through the window. Wid a feller.

SECOND CHILD:

    Was they doing it?

FIRST CHILD:

    He was riding her like Walter's dicky bird.

    QUILLER roars with pain or rage. It's difficult to tell which emotion.

QUILLER:

    Ye come back here.

CHILDREN:

    Killer Quiller! Killer Quiller!

    Their voices fade.

QUILLER:

    Come back here. I've an errand fer ye.

    He pauses. He bends down and picks up the Coke can. He looks at it.

I won't hurt ye. I wants to talk to ye.

    He looks at the can and moves as if to throw it, but hesitates. He looks at it again and goes and puts it under the day bed.

There'll be a bar fer ye . . . I still got bars.

    He pauses. He picks up the stones, one after the other and weighs them in his hand. He looks at them and drops them, almost gently, over the bridge. He pauses.

What do they know?

Bleakly.

What does any poor child know? They's no harm in
'em.

*A sweet voice begins to sing, off, slightly off-
key.*

MRS. IVANY:
Ye've got to kiss an angel good marnin'
An' love 'er like the devil when ye gits back 'ome . . .

*QUILLER stiffens, looks agitated and hurries
to the rail. He cranes over and looks. Suddenly,
he turns and looks in the direction of the windows.*

QUILLER:
Sadie! Sadie! They's no harm, maid. No harm. I
knows ye always did yer duty, maid, but they was
times, so they was, when ye preached me a sermon on
suffering . . .

MRS. IVANY: *suddenly stopping her humming*
Gerard! Gerard McGrath . . .

QUILLER: *gripping the rail and straining in the direction of
her voice* She's strong.

MRS. IVANY:
I seen ye pissin' on me turnips. Ye waits till I sees
yer mother.

QUILLER:
She's fine morals too.

He pauses.

It don't seem right. Her bendin' down over the turnips
like dat, legs warm in the earth, firm to the touch o'

the earth. Wet wi' the frost on the green leaves. And her wid no man. It don't seem right.

He is in turmoil. Suddenly, he staggers back and drops to his knees.

I knows, Lord. It ain't right. But ye made me whole, Lord, and all de parts were meant to be used. All of them. Even the private ones. And ye don't always want us to apologize fer the feelings ye gives us, does ye? . . .

He unclasps his hands and peers longingly underneath the rail in the direction of MRS. IVANY. Suddenly he sings.

"All t'ings bright and beautiful
All creatures great and small . . . "

He pauses, clasps his hands, and sits up.

Ye can see her, Lord. And I knows ye knows what I'm t'inkin', even though I knows ye be above t'inkin' such t'ings yerself. Dere's dat woman down there bendin' down amongst the turnips, wid a backside like a young pumpkin turned up to the sun. An' her man gone these t'ree years. Ye can see her same as me, Lord . . .

He unclasps his hands and peers beneath the rail. Again, he sings.

"All t'ings wild and wonderful
The good Lord made 'em all . . ."

He sits up and clasps his hands.

Ye've got to admit, 'tis a powerful sight.

He suddenly scrambles to his feet and leans out.

Mrs. Ivany. Mrs. Ivany.

To himself.

She heard. She's standing up. She's looking at me.

Wondering.

The wonder of it. Round and sweet. Firm to touch.

He shouts.

Mrs. Ivany. I got something fer ye here, maid.

He is excited. He swings one leg over the bridge, and sits as if he were astride a horse.

I got something fer ye, maid. Better 'n firmer dan dat ol' turnip. Come up here, maid. Come here.

MRS. IVANY: *off*
Fer the love o' God, will ye give over that foolishness, Uncle Quiller?

QUILLER: *jigging up and down excitedly on the rail*
It ain't foolishness. It ain't foolishness. It's joyful. It'd be holy. I'd tickle ye. Make ye laugh. We could sing hymns together while we was doing it . . .

"All t'ings bright and beautiful
All creatures great and small . . ."

NEIGHBOUR:
He's at it agin, Gladys.

MRS. IVANY:
Dirty ould divil. Woman's not safe in her own turnip patch these days. If it's not youngsters pissin' all over 'em, it's someone makin' ye dirty wid dere eyes.

NEIGHBOUR:
>Should be sent to the Mental. It'll be little girls next. Why don't someone take care of 'n, livin' in that big house all by hisself, lovely things in it too, and him touched ever since Aunt Sade died? Now that were a good woman.

MRS. IVANY:
>I'd go up and do a spell for him meself if he weren't so foolish, shouting at God and poor Sade, rest her soul. Do ye know he took it out onced and waved it at Mary Rose and she, unmarried? Ugliest and biggest t'ing she ever saw in her life, she said.

>*QUILLER has been listening intently.*

QUILLER:
>If I was to think it and not say it ye'd bloom in the night.

>*He gets down off the rail and paces agitatedly. He stops and leans over the rail.*

>I means no harm. I nivir done nobody any harm.

>*A pause. He shouts, stricken with some inner agony.*

>Let me in. Let me in to all the t'oughts of men rooted in ye, bloomin' like flowers!

>*A pause. A door slams, off.*

>We could pray together . . .

>*A cock crows. QUILLER looks off to the right.*

>Dat dicky bird must be blind or somet'in'.

>*He takes a pace to the left. He pauses and sings sadly.*

"All t'ings bright and beautiful
All creatures great and small . . ."

*He turns as if to go to the day bed. He sees the
ropes and he pauses. He goes up to the ropes and
pushes one of them. He catches it as it returns.
He pushes and catches it. Suddenly, he catches
hold of it and swings on it. He drops off on the
return. He chuckles and looks embarrassed. He
moves quickly to the right of the bridge and
peers out. He nods and hurries to the left of
bridge and looks out. He nods again. He looks to
the front. He looks back at the ropes. He rubs
his hands, spits on them, and suddenly, he
makes a run for a rope and jumps, catching it
swinging joyfully for a few seconds, singing at
the top of his lungs.*

"All t'ings bright and beautiful . . ."

*The rope breaks and he falls. He is sprawled out
on all fours, surprised, laughing, out of breath.*

Who'd a thought it.

He gets up laughing and wheezing.

Nivir thought I'd live to see it.

He goes to the day bed and sits.

Reckoned it'd be there when I were gone. When the
windows was gone. When the scavengers had took
what they would. Me friends.

He holds up a piece of rope.

Now it's gone before I.

*He moves to the front of the bridge and calls
out.*

61

Me rope's gone. The swing me and Sade made. When we was all just starting.

He holds up the piece of rope and pauses. He listens to the silence.

I could go and tell 'em, I suppose. I could walk down the street amongst 'em.

He looks at the piece of rope. He goes back slowly to the day bed.

Onced was when I was a part of 'em. And they was a part of me.

Puzzled.

I'm still here. And they is still there, but it ain't the same. I could . . . I could go amonst 'em.

He stands irresolute and goes to the door, where he pauses. He turns back.

I doesn't seem to want to leave somehow. Something might happen. Somebody come to call. Or them young divils heaving rocks at me windows.

A pause. He stands with the rope in his hand, head bowed in concentration. His reverie is broken by the explosive roar of a power saw. He starts and looks out. He moves rapidly to the front of the bridge. He shouts.

Good day, Jack.

The saw roars as it cuts, pauses and idles.

The rope broke.

He holds up the rope. The saw roars, cuts, idles.

Bine there since Sadie and me planned fer a family wot nivir came.

The saw roars, cuts, idles.

Dat's a nice bit o' wood.

The saw roars, cuts, idles.

Ye kin have me staircase when I've gone, Jack. I allus knowed ye were keen to have it. And the clapboard.

The saw roars, cuts, idles.

I'd sooner see the place used, if ye knows what I mean. Make me feel comfortable, rotting away as we does, to know someone were going up and down me stairs, keeping out the cold wid me clapboard.

The saw roars, cuts, idles.

Ye won't let 'em smash it up though, eh, Jack? Ye and the others. Me and Sade, we'd be sad to think of her all broken. Took down now, empty to the sky, the grass growing, bit o' green where we onced was . . . Dat's alright.

The saw roars, cuts, idles. QUILLER speaks urgently.

T'ings has got to be used, Jack. Not broken.

He calls.

Ye kin git in soon, Jack.

He pauses.

Ye wants to come up and talk about it?

The saw roars, sputters, and cuts out. There is
a silence. QUILLER slowly wanders to the left
and leans over the left rail.

Nice enough young fella, Jack. Works hard. Allus at
something. Like his fader. His woman give him
twenty-seven sons over the years. Nivir used to say
much, his fader didn't. Then Jack don't talk much
either. Come to think of it, nobody seems to talk as
much as they did. Or p'raps I jist don't hear 'em.

He becomes animated and walks quickly. He
bumps into the remains of the rope and starts.
He takes a pace forward.

Dat's it. They's speaking all the time and I doesn't
hear 'em. Must be gitting deaf or something. I should
'ave asked Luke to get me one o' they hearing aids,
I 'lows. They'd look better on me than him too. I
got ears for 'em to hook onto.

He notices that he is still carrying the broken
piece of rope. He experiments with it, looping it
behind his head and behind his ears. While he
is engaged in this, there is growing commotion,
off. A car passes and stops in the distance. There
is a confused babble of greeting. QUILLER sud-
denly hears the noise. In a quick gesture, he
throws the rope over the bridge, goes to the
front rail and peers out. He mutters.

My, my. Can't hardly see fer the dust.

He darts to the right of the bridge for a better
view. He becomes excited.

Why. 'Tis young George Bugden come 'ome from
them mines on the Labrador.

The babble off becomes louder. QUILLER, still
excited, runs to the left of the bridge.

Dey's all turning out to see him. And him driving a
car as big as a schooner.

He jumps up and down.

George. Hey, George, b'y.

The babble continues.

How is ye after all this time? Ye've grown some since
I last saw ye.

The babble continues.

Speak up, George, b'y. I can't hear ye.

>*He stops gesticulating suddenly. He leans out
>until it seems as if he must topple. With a quick
>movement, he gets back and paces agitatedly to-
>wards the door. He turns.*

She got no call to have gone and done that. Kissing
him in front of the world. She got no shame.

>*As if pushed from behind, reluctantly, he comes
>forward again.*

Still. He's well set up, I 'lows. And wid dat shiny
thing down there behind 'n he cuts quite the figure.

>*The babble begins to quiet down.*

I'd 've gone down to see 'n meself if it weren't for
Sadie.

>*He moves to the remains of the rope.*

Used to come here all the time, young George, him
and the others.

>*He pushes the rope.*

Creeping up through the garden to git at me plum trees.

He pushes the rope. He turns and goes to the front. He calls.

George . . . George, b'y. D'ye mind when ye'd come stealing me plums?

He laughs delightedly.

Me lying in wait for the sleveens in the outhouse, one eye to the peep-hole, and jest when dey was reaching up to grab a handful . . .

He laughs.

Fust time I scared young George so much he shit hisself. Fell right into a bed o' they stinging nettles, me roaring and chasing 'n wid dat old rape hook I kept in the outhouse fer cleaning me nails . . .

He leans out.

George, b'y. George.

A pause.

Gone. Dey's all gone. Just dat thing there sitting in the middle of the road.

He pauses.

I expect he'll be up the once to see me.

He pauses.

'Spect they'll all be up by and by.

He goes slowly back to the day bed and lies down. He shuts his eyes, and sings with the strength of loneliness.

"Will your anchor hold in the storms of life,
When the clouds unfold . . ."

He stops and sits up.

They got their own back though. Aye. I minds it now. Burnt me punt on bonfire night. Nivir the divil could prove they did it, but I knowed right enough. Nice lookin' punt. I mind now the big spruce I cut fer the heel of her. Curved like a bow. Or a . . . a . . .

He closes his eyes to contain the unspoken and painful image. He opens his eyes again.

It wor raining dat day. Come on after first light. Wispy old clouds hanging to the tops of the trees.

Wondering.

And I but seventeen then. Seventeen.

He pauses.

Sweet God.

He pauses.

Seventeen.

He pauses.

'N the water dropping slow offen the trees and everything full of the sound of the water. And dere he were. Big old spruce taller be ten feet than all the trees around 'n. And someone had made a mark in the bark. It must have been when the tree wor growin' fer the marks were nearly gone, but ye could

67

see it wor a young fella's name and a girl's, wid an arrow through 'em. And they was a curve in her bigger 'n me old cow's tits when they was bustin' wi' milk. Jest the t'ing fer the heel. I felt a bit bad about cuttin' her, but that wor only because of the names and they probably long gone. And, as I told 'n, you'll be alive this years yet, in the water, holding me up. And I s'pose, when they took her like that, in a prank, it wor dat day taken out of me. They burnt dat day out o' me life and I nivir knew it until now. And young George has brung it back to me in that shiny new car.

He gets off the day bed and kneels, clasping his hands.

Lord. Lord, is you listenin'? You've a powerful long memory and ye does work in a strange way, like de hymn says. I'd like to thank ye fer giving me dat day back, Lord.

He waits for a reply.

But 'tis strange you should give it back now.

He listens.

No, Lord. I's not questioning ye. Jest telling ye how I feels. That's all.

He gets up and goes to the left. He peers up at the sky.

Sun be high.

He blinks and rubs his hands across his eyes.

Powerful fer the time o' year.

From this moment on, the lighting must empha-size the alternate confusion and clarity that illuminates QUILLER's experience. The light now becomes intense, the arc lights flooding the film of his memory, and then begins to narrow in focus until beyond the confines of the bridge everything is in a tangible dark. The light of inner revelation is balanced against the blind window of the external world.

He begins to walk back across the bridge. He pauses and rubs his eyes. He shakes his head and begins to sing.

"Will your anchor hold in the storms of life,
When the clouds unfold their wings of strife,
When the strong tides lift and the cables strain . . ."

The hymn falters. QUILLER looks puzzled. He goes forward and looks out over the bridge into the blackness. Suddenly, he turns and goes quickly into the house. He is gone for sixty seconds. He returns with a mug of tea and goes anxiously to the front of the bridge. He peers out. He looks at his tea. He crosses to the day bed. He puts the tea down and goes back to the front of the bridge. He peers out again. He turns and goes quickly into the house for another. Sixty seconds. He returns with a bowl, towel and shaving gear as he had at the opening of the play. He repeats the exact same actions that he did earlier, prior to shaving. He lathers his brush and raises it to his face. He stops and wonders. He feels his face with his other hand.

Did I do this afore today?

He rubs his face vigorously.

If I did it, weren't too good a job, Lord.

He peers out over the bridge into the darkness. The light blasts his eyes. He puts down the brush and rubs his eyes. He shakes his head.

What did I do today?

He pauses.

I got something to do today. Don't rightly know what it is.

He pauses.

Don't rightly know what day it is.

The lights blasts his eyes. He rubs his face then starts, as if in, or proceeding into a dream.

I knows . . .

He peers out again.

Must be gone four-t'irty, though 'tis powerful dark fer the time o' yar. I'd best git on.

With brisk, almost youthful movements, he picks up the razor and goes back to the door, whistling cheerfully the air, "Will Your Anchor Hold." He kneels and begins to carve out on the door: QUILLER LAITE, Anno Domini 1900-19 . . ." He carves it out in such a way that the door resembles a headstone. He whistles as he works, and then, still carving, as if in response to a voice, he says . . .

'Marnin', Amos. 'Tis a bit early for ye to be out, isn't it? And ye nigh crippled with them arthritic bones. Dey's a mist on the water. It'll torment ye . . .

He nods at the reply and works away.

I'm doing a breast plate . . .

He works away.

I dunno, b'y. Skipper Eli's eldest wor killed last night by the train, up in the woods there. I nivir t'ought the t'ing were fast enough to kill a rabbit . . .

He listens, nods and works away.

Oh, aye. Went to sleep on it, did he? On de tracks. Allus did have a hard head, that one. How's Eli taking it?

He listens, nods and works.

She did? Last night? Jes like the cow, that one, drop 'n and walk on. Oh well, the Lord giveth, the Lord taketh away. How many's that now?

He listens, nods and works away.

Twenty-four borned, nineteen living now, Lord jumpin' and here's me and Sade wore out wi' trying. Ain't no sense to it at all.

He listens and nods.

Aye. Ye can drop me a fish off on yer way back, if ye've a mind. Take care now . . .

He has finished. He steps back and admires his work. Suddenly, he takes a pace back. He looks at it amazed, then looks at the razor.

Dat's me. Dat's me own door. And dis is my razor.

Appalled, with a roar, he hurls the razor off to the left. He kneels and peers at his work again, then clasps his hands.

Lord.

He shouts.

Lord. Kin ye hear me? If ye wouldn't mind . . . No. No, b'y, that's a poor start.

He pauses and contains himself.

Look here, Lord . . .

He pauses.

No, that's too bossy by far.

He tries again.

Lord. Fer the love of Jesus, will ye tell me what's going on?

He cocks his ear.

I'm waiting, Lord.

He cocks his ear again.

Lord, I've sailed wid ye all me life, even when I weren't sure where ye was leading me.

He pauses.

And now I'm confused, Lord. T'ings is different. But they is the same.

Strongly.

I've ruined me razor, Lord. I've trown it away. Is ye trying to tell me not to shave anymore or what? . . .

The bridge is bathed in the reflected glow of flames. QUILLER leaps to his feet.

What in the name of? . . .

He runs to the right of the bridge and looks out.
He shouts.

Amos . . . Amos . . .

A cacophony of sounds filter through space,
flames crackle. Wind, cries of lamentation, a
church organ resolve into a congregation singing
slowly, painfully . . .

"Will your anchor hold in the sea of life,
When the clouds unfold their wings of strife,
When the strong tides lift and the cables strain,
Will your anchor drift or firm remain?"

The sounds stop. Flames flicker on QUILLER's
face.

Ye ould divil.

He pauses.

Ye knew all the time. Lighting the fire in the midship
room. Catching the fish. The last supper. Falling into
the flames. Dead, falling into the flames.

The flames still flicker on QUILLER's face.

Drifting on fire on the water. Dead and burning on
the water. Smile like a baby on yer face.

The flames die down. The light narrows, becomes
more intense on the door and the day bed. It
begins to dim on the other areas.

QUILLER shakes his head. He hits his head with
his fist. Quickly, he goes to the centre where he
peers out. Then, he goes to the left, which is
almost in darkness.

It's like the t'ings what's gone and the t'ings what are all mixed up.

He goes to the centre.

It were this marnin' I were woke by **Walter's dicky bird.**

He pauses.

But then I bin woke every marnin' fer years **by** Walter's dicky bird.

He pauses and feels his face.

And I did shave this marnin'. But then, I bin **shaving** every marnin' dis lifetime since I wor a man.

He looks out anxiously.

And Amos! Amos, he bin gone these twenty year. **Yit** I could've sworn I wor talkin' to 'n, dat I saw 'n **agin** like on dat marnin', drifting into the dawn light, like . . . like a piller o' fire on the water.

He pauses and in a small tired voice says . . .

What am I to make of it at all?

He goes and sits slowly on the day bed. He sits there for a moment in silence.

I 'lows He's left me. After all dis time. Lord? . . . Lord? . . .

He calls out in a whisper and listens.

No. They's nobody there . . .

He bows his head and sits in silence. The sound of low laughter, off, is heard in the blackness . . .

A man and a woman. QUILLER stirs. The laughter becomes louder. He leaps to his feet.

'Tis her. 'Tis her, I swear . . .

He runs up and down excitedly, peering this way and that. The laughter repeats itself, reverberates almost. QUILLER sees the source. He stops, agonized.

My God. In me own garden. She brung him down here to do it in front of me. To shame me.

He casts around for something to throw and sees the bowl. He hurls it into the darkness. Then, the towel and the shaving brush. The laughter is heard again. Desperate, he spies his mug by the day bed. He goes to it and hurls it too into the blackness. He roars.

I kin see ye. I kin see ye. Going to it like a smelly old nanny goat. I tell ye . . . I tell ye I got something better 'n . . . I got somethin' . . .

As swiftly as it has come, the rage leaves him. He pauses, bewildered.

I don't believe what I'm saying.

He pauses.

What I'm saying wid me mout' isn't what's here.

He touches his heart. He creeps up to the rail and looks out. He clambers softly onto the rail and standing, clutching the roof for support, he speaks . . .

Aye. Dat's it. Hold tight now. 'Tis a long night. Moon'll be up by and by, creeping up out of the mist. Big on the water.

He nods and smiles.

I'll ask the Lord to bless ye wid babies.

Still hanging onto the roof, he looks up.

Lord. Dis is me. Is dat you, Lord? I'd like fer ye to bless that union what's taking place in me garden. They's down there, Lord. Mrs. Ivany and young George, over by the raspberry canes. I's tellin' ye in case yer mist is making things a bit difficult fer ye. Ye will bless 'em. Lord.

> *He listens and, as if receiving a reply, he smiles seraphically. He nods and clambers down. As he walks back from the bridge rail towards the day bed, the light behind him dies. He pauses and turns.*

"Will your anchor hold . . ."

> *He stops and remembers something. He looks up in the direction of the window.*

It wor a bit like that wi' us, weren't it, Sadie?

> *He crosses to the door, opens it and calls up.*

Sadie. Sadie, girl. D'ye want yer tay now?

> *He listens.*

Shall I bring ye a biscuit?

> *He listens, shakes his head and feels in his long johns. He produces the biscuit bag and takes one out. He begins to munch it, standing by the door. He puts the bag back inside his long johns.*

I hardly remembers a t'ing ye says, Sadie. P'raps that's just as well.

He munches.

I minds the way ye looked now when I fust saw ye stooping down amongst the turnips.

He pauses, puzzled, troubled by a recollection. He shakes his head.

It were fall. Frost still on the leaves. Yer legs was wet with fall. And we coming back to this house, after the shotguns and the dancing.

He pauses.

Walked up alone . . .

He pauses.

No moon, I recalls. Jest a few stars on the water . . .

He pauses.

And then working . . . Six months to the woods and coming home, ye wid yer arms white wid flour.

He pauses.

Three months to the ice and coming home to ye, wid yer arms white wid flour.

He pauses.

Eight months on the schooner, Boston, the West Indies, Brazil. And coming home to ye, yer arms white wid flour.

He pauses.

Nivir full o' child though.

He finishes his biscuit.

P'raps we sinned. Though I doesn't know how. I wouldn't do it again.

Vehemently.

Not again. Leave yer so long and so often. P'raps that were it. I'd not ever 'ave bin around long enough to be a fader to 'n. Until he wor growed. Too late then, I 'lows.

He pauses.

I wishes I could mind what ye said though.

He pauses.

But I s'pose that's the way of it.

> *He shuts the door slowly. The light blazes on the inscription. He walks slowly back towards the day bed. The only areas lit now are the day bed and the door. He sits and sings.*

"It will surely hold in the floods of death
When the waters cold chill our latest breath . . . "

He stops.

Lord, Lord. Ye knows something. Dat hymn's brung it back to me. All dese years since Amos died I've been troubled. Didn't make sense, ye see . . .

He sings.

"On the rising tide it can never fail . . ."

He stops.

Amos. He knew it made no sense. No dust fer he. No worms fer him either. No graves filling up wit' water soon as they was dug. No bumping to eternity . . .

no offence, Lord . . . In the back of a pick-up. Ye've got to admit, Lord, 'tis not very dignified. Six good neighbours wid a load on stumbling up the hill to the cemetery were more dignified than that old Chevy rattling up the hill, enough to shake the bones out of ye afore ye had a chanced to turn at all. No.

> On the water.
> Fire on the water.
> And yer own boat.
> And a couple o' cod for company.

He sings.

"We shall anchor fast by the heavenly shore . . ."

He stops, excited.

We ain't dust, Lord. That's what it is. I've bin foolish. P'raps dat's why they leaves me alone all the time. Talking to ye. Offering . . . forgive me . . . me poor ould sex to Mrs. Ivany. Getting stuck in me own head. Me own time.

He pauses.

Dey all talked to me afore I talked to Ye. Afore Sadie took to her bed.

He pauses.

I s'pose, Lord, I let ye down after all. Made ye a figure of fun t'rough me. It weren't me intention though. P'raps I's not quite right in the head. Lonely, I 'lows.

He chuckles.

Quiller Laite, born 1900 . . .

He pauses.

A logging man. A fishing man. Songs in the bunk-house. Under the rigging.

Hymns on the water. Alone on the water.
Sadie and the house spotless.
Sadie alone and the house spotless.
No sound.
Jest the sound o' tears sometimes.
Jest the floor sometimes peckedy wid her tears.

Wondering.

And all of it . . .
The nights and the days of it . . .
Jest to find out we ain't dust.

Dat's a powerful piece of knowledge ye give me, Lord, even though I don't deserve it after the way I treated ye.

He pauses.

I got to let them know, Lord. I got to share it . . .

He makes no attempt to rise. He shouts.

Mrs. Ivany. George. Jack . . . They's nothing to worry about no more. We ain't dust. We's all fire and water . . .

He shouts after a pause.

Jack. Jacky, b'y.

He falls back on the day bed, stretches out, folds his hands and sings.

"Will your anchor hold in the storms of life . . ."

There is a silence. The unmistakable sound of footsteps is heard in the house. The door opens

80

slowly. There is nobody there. Not moving,
QUILLER speaks . . .

I've fergotten yer tay, maid. I'm dat excited. I 'as
to tell ye, though I 'lows it might have made no difference. We ain't dust, Sadie. We're all fire and water.
We ain't dust after all . . .

Silence. He doesn't move. The light fades on
him. It shines on the open door, then fades there
too.

PRODUCTION NOTES

In another play, *Jacob's Wake*, the Skipper says at one point that "a house is a ship." This is not mere fancy. The association between ships and houses in Newfoundland is very strong, and thus, in the outports, most houses have a "bridge;" the landsmens equivalent is a verandah or a porch or a raised patio. But the analogy doesn't stop there. Many still speak of "going to bunk" at bedtime. The furnishings of such a "bridge" are fairly standard, as in the play. A day bed, and occasionally, a rocking chair. Quite frequently, there is also a swing suspended from the bridge beams.

The hymn, "Will Your Anchor Hold in the Storms of Life?" was written by Miss Priscilla J. Owens, who was born a minister's daughter in Cornwall in 1829 and of whom, alas, little else is known. Many of the great Methodist hymns of which this is one are inspired with an evangelical fervour related directly to the profound mysteries of physical labour observed, but often not experienced by the writer, as in this case — poverty, passion, pain, loss, the lifestyle of the Apostles manifest amongst the deprived. The ability to translate the metaphors of daily life into a sung Christian vocabulary was one of the energizing forces of the early Methodist movement, a vocabulary vigorously sustained by many Quillers on the east coast of Newfoundland. The difference between Charley Pride's "You've Got to Kiss an Angel Good Morning" and "All Things Bright and Beautiful" is merely one of tone.

In production, it was found that the carving of the breast plate upon the door created some technical problems, the least of which was providing a new door every night. A solution practiced with some success was to have the motif pre-carved, filled with putty or some similar substance, and painted over. The actor then scrapes out the putty with the razor. There are possibly other solutions, but this one appears to work.

Terese's Creed

The lights rise on THERESE's kitchen. There are no containing flats; shape and structure are suggested by pieces of two by four. The artifacts, not the surroundings, must dominate our attention.

A tub washer sits downstage left. Behind it, centre, there is a sink. A black plastic pipe drains the water beneath the house. A kitchen chrome set, table and chairs, occupies the area right. It is littered with debris from a family breakfast. From one of the pieces of two by four, there hangs a wall phone. The others may contain outlets for appliances. Extreme left, there may be the suggestion of a porch which leads to the entrance. On the porch there are four or five ten gallon plastic buckets filled with water. Extreme right, there is a shelf big enough to contain an electric kettle and a canister. A mug or two is attached to one of the exposed ribs of the kitchen.

THERESE is a largish woman in her mid-forties.

*Although the strain of raising a large family on
a fisherman's income shows in her face and in
the occasional weariness that overcomes her,
she has much energy and fire. Her eyes still
project the image of a young girl on occasions.*

*As the play opens, she is shouting from the
doorway at her departing children.*

THERESE:

Marvin . . . Marvin . . . Ye hear me now. Stop in to
Miss Millie's on yer way back from school and keep
her company fer a bit.

She pauses.

I don't give a shit what ye wants to do, boy, do as yer
told. Bernice . . .

In a shrill voice.

Bernice . . . Stop to Cull's, will ye, an' bring me a
pound o' bolony. And don't ye go charging no more
cookies to me account . . . I'm wise to ye, girl. Yis,
and tell her I'll be in to settle on Sat'day.

*The sound of a school bus drawing up is heard.
There are distant shouts, then the bus draws
away. THERESE comes in from the porch area.
She pushes her hair out of her eyes.*

Oh my. Some days . . . Well, I'd best git on.

*She crosses to the washer, takes out the lead,
together with a box of detergent and a plastic
bleach bottle. She plugs the lead into an outlet,
crosses to the porch, brings in a ten gallon pail
of water and, with an effort, lifts it and empties
it into the tub. She takes the bucket back to the
porch, half fills it from another bucket, then
returns and empties that bucket into the washer*

84

as well. She then pours some detergent into the washer.

Dat's a blessed relief now, washing in cold water. Times I'd spend half the day trying to heat enough to do one washer load . . .

She adds some bleach, then crosses to the outlet.

'Tis already plugged in. I swears, I'll fergit me head next.

She turns on the washer. Its strange, regular thumping sound is reminiscent of a heartbeat. She puts the lid on to stop the water splashing out and goes downstage to look out.

And it'll rain now, I suppose, and me with neither clothes clean fer the youngsters and it graduation in a few days . . .

She disappears upstage into the darkness and emerges almost immediately with a huge arm- load of clothes. She dumps them down and begins to sort them out; whites in one pile, coloureds in another.

Though why I should bother about 'em graduating, the Lord only knows. Sometimes I thinks 'tis only foolishness. If their father were alive now, it might be different.

She loads the washer with the whites and puts the lid on.

And 'tis not as if they even care what they does wi' their life. Time was when they was no choices. We nivir had no choice. If ye was a boy ye got thrown into manhood afore ye was wet behind the ears, no matter how hard the mothers prayed fer 'em to be something other than fishermen, walking the water everyday. And we . . .

She laughs.

I minds me mother to this day. I wor coming up fifteen an' it wor as close as she ever come to giving me a lesson on the facts o' life. Weren't necessary, I suppose. We all knew what we had to be be the time we was nine or ten. Aye. I wor gitting ready to leave school dat year. Grade 8, I wor in. Stopped me one morning as I wor about to step through the door. Looks at me long and hard an' nods, satisfied. "Ye're alright, maid," she said. "Ye'll do. Ye're good looking enough to git a good man, not like some wi' squish mout's and eyes that had to settle fer a man old enough to be their fathers, aye, and ye're not dat beautiful as ye'd catch all and mebbe none be the end o' it."

She laughs again.

No. We 'ad no choice, none at all. Mebbe 'tis a good thing . . . Though I'm sure I don't know anymore what's good and what isn't fer anybody.

She crosses to the table, sits, pours herself a cup of tea and lights a cigarette. She's not really used to them. It's a habit she's picked up recently out of a sense of bravado or simply defiance, a wish to do something which has met with disapproval from her family all her life. She puffs like a teenager.

I suppose we never had time to think neither. Work afore school, work after in the house, then helping wi' the fish or about the gardens. Git out once in a while fer a walk on a Sat'day, get to a dance mebbe. Meet some young feller ye've known all yer life but somehow 'tis different, and him wit' eels in his feet an' the Divil's grin an' a look would turn yer stomach

to water and there ye is . . . staring up at the stars
one night and him doing whatever he wants and
knowing 'tis all writ up dere in dem stars from dat
time on. The journey to the altar an' the swelling
stomach an' the round o' cooking and washing and
making fish and cutting wood an' berry picking in the
fall. And den the work gits in the way o' the play
till it seems there never was none, no, an' it be useless
to grieve fer, as the priest says, we's only born to
work and sorrow in dis life. I mustn't mind though,
'tis not all been a torment, and I had it better than
me mother an' dey, dat's a fact. I minds her telling
me once about me being borned. She wor helping me
grandfather on the stage, me father wor gone to the
Labrador dat year. All I minds of him now is the
smell o' tobaccy and the hard voice when he spoke,
and dat weren't often. She begun to feel the pains
right strong, and her water broke, right dere on the
stage head. "I got to go, Father," she tells 'n. "Christ,
maid," he says. "What fer?" "To born the baby,"
she says. He grunts den, and after a bit says, "If ye
must, ye must, I suppose, but don't ye be too long."
An' she pushed herself up the path to the house, and
Mary Ellen come den as had borned most of us and
me mother had the hot water and the towels laid out
be the time she got up an I wor just about t'rough.
Dat wor morning. Be the time the day had done wor'
out she wor back again wi' him on the stage. Feared
to deat' o' him, she were. But my, she had beautiful
hair. Black, it wor. Right down to her arse. I minds
playing wi' it as a girl, combing it for her. She sitting
and rocking be the old stove, half crooning to herself,
and me brushing, brushing till her head gleamed, and
it didn't seem to belong in dat crowded little house.
Wood smoke an' the smell o' dried fish and me grandfather's tobaccy . . . Target, it wor . . . dat belonged.
But not me mother's hair, it wor like something in
books. Something in dreams a long time ago. I minds
right up to the time she wor dying . . . It wor streaked
wi' grey den, but still long and thick . . . she'd wish
fer me to do her hair. "D'ye minds when it wor all

black, girl," she'd say . . ."All shining . . . And ye'd
sit an' do me hair on a summer's evening."

She pauses.

It wor like another part o' her dat never belonged to
the dried fish, the wood smoke, the labour at the
stage head. Mine wor nivir like dat. More like me
father's, I s'pose. Stringy, tough. Pat used to tell me
'twere like a witches broom.

She laughs and pats her hair.

She told me her hair come from her mother. She wor
supposed to have had the most beautiful hair in the
whole of Ireland but it fell out on the ship coming
over . . . Some disease or other, I don't mind which it
wor now. Till the day she died, she wor a bandana.
Even when they laid her out, she had on a bandana.
Red, wi' white spots on it. Foolish, the way some
t'ings sticks in yer head. Oh my. Dis won't git me
nowhere, I suppose.

> *She gets up and crosses to the washer and turns
> it off. She crosses to the porch, comes back with
> a large plastic bowl which is used as a washing
> basket. She puts it down and begins to take
> garments from the washer and put them through
> the wringer.*

I suppose I'll keep going now till dey's all gone.
'Tis a strange business. Ye spends yer life raising a
fambly, an' just when dey seems ready to be friends
dey's off and running like the Divil was at their
tail. Dat's how it was wi' the others anyway and I
doubt dem dat's left'll be much different. And when
dey's gone, where are ye? Alone in a house full o'
empty bedrooms and chipped dishes and a few
pictures stuck on the cabinet to remind ye of where
yer life went. If Pat wor alive now, I suppose t'ings
'd be a mite different. I don't know though. Seems

like he knew all along it wor hardly worth it. "It'd
be nice, maid," he said . . .

She pauses and struggles with the memory.

"It'd be nice . . ."

She pauses again.

Dat's right. Come on to snow in the evening . . .
First snow o' the winter, and it blowing strong from
the nor' east enough to freeze the marrow of ye. I
allus hates to see that first snow . . . 'Tis like the
winter settling down on yer like an ould coffin lid
and ye still alive, banging away inside.

She pauses. The wringer grinds on.

'Tis such a short time afore the snows come.

*The wringer continues to grind on. She breaks
from her memories with a start.*

Oh my, dere I goes again . . .

*She delves into the tub for more clothes to put
through the wringer and comes up with BER-
NICE's bra and panties. She holds them up and
pauses.*

And I don't suppose she'll be long now afore she's at
it . . . If she isn't already. Blessed Virgin, 'tis a worry.
She but fifteen and dey thinks I don't know how
they feels or what dey does, only now 'tis the backs
o' cars and not down be the stage head or up on the
hills o' nights. And wi' Pat gone and her big brothers,
I doesn't seem able to hold her. Seems like wi' no
men at home dey goes crazy. We allus held off till
the last minute, till we was sure of 'em. And ye can
be sure we was den, fer if ye got into trouble, an'
most of us did it seems, then it wor between famblies.

. . . Got nothing to do with ye or he at all and whether ye wanted to or no, it was up to the altar wi' ye, girl. Ye've made yer bed and now ye must lie on it. Aye, and even afore dat, if ye confessed it, and ye knows ye had no choice about dat either, den the priest would ask when ye was coming to see'n about the banns, and dat after giving ye enough penance to keep ye on yer knees for a week. We t'ought we was free, but ach, we was no better off then an ould cod . . . Everywhere ye runs dey's a trap somewhere. And we too foolish to mind'n or look where we was going at all. I doesn't know about Bernice though.

She puts BERNICE's clothes through the wringer and fishes in the washer for some more.

Times change and dey ain't nothing anyone can do about dat. But I knows dey got no thought o' marriage, or be spoken fer it anyways. I got her life threatened. "Don't ye come home to me, Missy," I tells her, "pregnant, because I'm not raisin' no more youngsters." "I knows what I'm doing," she says, saucy as a black. "Yis, maid," I tells her, an' I too knows what yer doing wi' that Sam Pollock, and him a Protestant." In my day ye had to confess dat too, if ye talked to a Protestant, dat's if ye were alive to tell the tale after yer father or yer brothers found out. "Why, mam," she says, laughing to me face, "yer some old fashioned. Nobody cares fer dem things anymore, only old Father Sullivan and he's too foolish to talk about." "Ye minds yer mout'," I tells her, "talking of a priest dat way." Ah, but dey got no respect fer nothing dese days. An' I suppose dey don't care who's who or what's what and dat's a good thing in some ways fer as I minds it, it wor always causing trouble one way or another. But the way dey carries on, her and dem like her, dat's what's foolish fer they've all their lives running ahead o' 'em and all it takes is to open yer legs once too often fer a feller who doesn't give a good goddamn fer anything, let alone ye, and dey's half of it gone, an' the shame of it on ye, and the pain of it on ye, too soon be half, and yer girlhood gone like a flower cut wi' the frost.

She turns off the wringer, and fills the washer again. She puts the lid on and switches it on. She picks up the bowl of clean clothes and moves to the doorway.

Well, drat dat. 'Tis raining cats and dogs and me wi' a full washer load yit. I knows I should a' done it yestiday, but oh my, me back wor some bad.

She crosses the kitchen to the extreme right and unhooks a pulley rope from one of the pieces of two by four. A clothes rack lowers. She fastens the rope and begins to load the clothes onto the rack.

I should git down to the doctor wid'n, I suppose, but they're some stunned. All dey wants to do is poke around in yer privates, scrape dis, scrape dat, and what the Lord dat's got to do wi' me back, I don't know, unless it comes from spending too much time on it as a maid.

She laughs.

I'm some shocking . . . Mary Francis now, me eldest daughter, she's always on about it. "Ye needs a hysterectomy," she says, whatever dat is. Ever since she married dat teacher feller from the mainland, she's got right bossy. "Yer draining away," she says, "dey'll be nothing left o' ye be the time yer fifty." "So what," I says, "ye'll all be gone den and what should I care."

She arranges some more clothes.

Though if Bernice gits herself into trouble, I suppose I'll be kept busy fer a bit . . . They'll be something to keep me . . . Oh, but dat's a terrible way to think. I suppose they means well. And worried, I allow, about being left to care fer me, but I tells dem I'll take care o' meself until me time comes, like Miss Millie.

She hauls up the rack and once again goes to the table and lights up a cigarette.

And den when Jack, me eldest, wor home last on leave from the Forces, all o'em was at me to git married again.

She laughs.

"Yer still good looking, mam," they says.

She laughs again, self consciously, and smoothes down her hair.

Yis, I suppose I am, hair like a witches broom, having borned ten youngsters wi' eight living, thanks be to God. An' what would I be doing wi' another man? They was ever only one man fer me, and it might sound foolish to dem dese days. Sure, they has more men be the time dey's twenty than Patsy O'Hare and dey says she took on the whole fishing fleet one season . . . Dat was afore Father McCarthy got a holt to her and she seen the light and went to become a nun.

She pauses.

It do git a bit lonely in bed at night times. When ye just want to talk or turn in to the feel o' a man, the smell o' him. The hardness o' him, legs like an old spruce, hard and bent from a lifetime balancing on boats. I has Bernice in now fer company, but 'tis not the same. Times when I 'as to turn from her, when I feels like crying.

She pauses. A tear gathers in the corner of her eye. She wipes it with her sleeve.

Ach. Give over dat old foolishness, maid, the days in full o' work yit, and ye didn't have it as hard as yer mother and dey, suppose yer man has upp'd and gone. He wor good to ye while he wor alive, according to his lights, and dat's more dan some kin say . . . But I'll not be marrying agin. Dat's all gone now . . . Dat part o' me is all gone now and if I does hunger sometimes . . . 'tis soon passed.

The phone rings, a startling, loud sound. She puts out her cigarette and crosses to the phone.

Hello . . . Yis, maid, I'm doing a bit o' wash, but the Lord knows when I'll git it dry . . . It do. Well, I might get it out by an' by den.

She pauses.

Yes, I did see it.

She pauses.

Well, I'd kill dat. I've never seen the like fer cheating on a maid.

She pauses.

No, girl, I don't think she will. But if 'twas me, I'd leave'n, an' dat's a fact.

She pauses.

I knows, maid, some crooked, dat one wi' all her money. What good does it do 'em? If I wor to turn like dat when I got old, I'd give up.

She pauses.

Oh, she's canny though. She's trying to git her hooks into dat lawyer, I kin see that. He'd better watch hisself.

She pauses.

True enough, girl . . . butter wouldn't melt in her mout', but he must be some stunned if he can't see t'rough the sherry and cookies she serves him.

She pauses.

I don't know who killed 'n, maid, I'm sure. But I knows the young feller didn't do it. Ye kin tell be his face. My, he's some good-looking.

She pauses and laughs.

I dare say I wouldn't push him out o' bed, maid.

She pauses.

Push him to the wall? . . .

She laughs.

Ye're some shocking. Well, alright den.

She pauses.

I might . . . Ye kin give me a call later . . . Oh . . . Lill, how's yer mother?

She pauses.

She is?

She pauses.

I heard tell of a feller down the motel was selling silver medals fer dat.

She pauses.

Ye wears it all the time, maid, and it's supposed to
be just wonderful fer the arthritis . . . Well, ye knows
how crippled Big Mick wor, his hands jest like pig's
knuckles. Well, he's been wearing one dis week, and
Mary says she's nivir seen him looking so spry dis
years. He wor out chopping wood fer her yestiday.

She pauses.

Dat's true enough too . . . I told her yestiday she'd
have to watch'n. Next thing the nosey old welfare
officer'll be round telling 'n to git to work, ye knows
how dey is. Yis, well alright, maid. I'll talk to ye later.

*She hangs up the phone and crosses to the
washer, turning it off,. She starts the wringer
and begins to put the clothes through it.*

I jest loves that Edge o' Night. Only bit o' time I
'as to meself all day, jest afore the youngsters come
home. I used to watch dat Fambly Court all the time
too, but sure 'tis not like a court at all. I nivir seen a
judge like dat one . . . Puffing away at dat stinking
old pipe, and acting like God the Father Almighty on
a good day when everyone knows he's 'as bad days
like the rest o' us. I minds when I 'ad to go up dat
time wi' Walter, when he wor caught bringing dat
caribou home. Pat wor some proud o' him, and him
but thirteen. "Don't ye mind dem, boy," he says.
"Bunch o' idiots, dat's what dey is. What do dey want
to bring dem beasts to the island fer if it's not to gi'
folks a chanct o' a meal o' meat now and agin? Aye,
and meat dey can't afford to buy, fer the price dey
pays fer fish be not enough to keep a scarecrow alive.
Dey can rob a poor man blind," he says, "but God
help dose what tries to help theyselves and keep off'n
the Welfare." "S'pose they means to keep 'em fer
damn tourists," he said.

She pauses.

Funny really . . . Pat wor like dat. Speak to the Divil in his own house, not afeard o' man nor beast, but the minute he got t'rough the door, it wor like he wor a different man. Do anything to avoid trouble. It'd be, "Yes, sir. Good morning, sir," an' dey doing terrible tings to 'n, cheating him on his fish and charging too much fer his gear, yit on the water he wor like a lion. I've niver seen him afeard . . . No, and dey was times I was wid'n, when I wor younger, helping him haul the traps, I t'ought the sea would swallow us up fer sure an' him whistling away, not giving a damn. He wor never happier dan when he wor on the water. Seemed like the boat wor a part o' him, and he and the boat wor a part o' the water. I suppose he wor free den. That was it. He never knowed dat dat wor when I loved'n most. And dat's the time, I suppose, when he niver cared what or who I wor as long as I kept me place and did as I wor told.

She pauses.

But just let'n walk out o' the house . . .

She wrings a few more clothes and pauses again.

He nivir went to the court wi' Walter. I 'ad to go. And the old feller on the bench . . . Well, I nivir seen such a miserable looking creature in all me life . . . He looked like a sculpin 'ad bin pickled in brine fer a week. And pickled . . . I suppose dat's what he wor . . . Ye could smell him all over the court house. An' when our time come he called me up, not Walter. "Yer son was caught flagarente delicto," he says. "Does ye know what dat means?" Now where in the name of all dat's holy had I bin all me life to know what dat meant. "No, sir," I says. Saucy, I wor. "And I doesn't think I want to know." He gets nasty then. "Yer son is a minor, Mrs. Moriarty," he says, "and therefore ye're responsible fer his crime."

"And what crime is dat, Your Honour?" I asks.
"We've a house full o' mout's to feed and little
enough to manage on, an' he acted like a man to git
some meat fer us." Dere was some tittering in court,
den I tells ye and he banged with the hammer something fierce, den made a face as if it hurt'n . . . I
'low, he had a hangover, fer he wor to the Merchants
the night afore and ye may be sure they weren't
short of a drop dere . . . Planning what to do wi' us
all, I expect . . . Walter and his caribou, and dem as
'adn't paid dere bills and the few what got into fights.
"'Tis stealing, mam," he says to me. "Dat caribou is
the property of the Crown, and in any case, yer son
'ad no licence." "We can't afford no licence, sir,"
I says then, "and I doubts if the Queen'd come all
the way from Buckingham Palace or wherever it
is she's to, to check on one skinny caribou . . . "Sure,"
I says, "dey's hardly enough grass here to feed dat,
'tis a mortal sin to let'n roam. Uncle Jack Penton
now, he found the bones o' t'ree of 'm on the upper
side of the arm, starved to death dey was." Well, the
court was going some, I tell ye, and some were cheer-
ing and shouting out and he got redder 'n a turkey
in the face. "No doubt he did," he shouts. "No
doubt. And I don't doubt but the meat dat was on
dem bones 'ad already found its way into the Moriarty stomachs, and dem like ye for dere's no caribou
living," he says, "couldn't live in dem barrens with
all the moss and lichen dat's up there." "Fined
twenty five dollars," he says. "And bound
over to keep the peace in your charge, mam."

She laughs.

Twenty five dollars! I asked 'n den, meek and mild
like, if I could pay it off be the week. He softened at
dat and asked what I 'ad in mind. "Ten cents, sir,"
I said. And he banging away wi' that old hammer
again and wincing, and shouting fer the Mountie to
clear the court. Well, the upshot o' it was dat all o'
Walter's fishin' money went to pay 'n off dat year.

And Pat, when he heard what I done, he laughed.
Den he swore on me fer shaming 'n. Den he laughed
agin. Funny though, how he wouldn't go. The sea and
the creatures in it . . . Dat wor the only world fer
him. The rest o' it wor a millstone . . . Aye, and me
too at times. He told me once he hated me. That wor
later, mind, when they didn't seem much laughter
left in 'n. I took dat some hard, I tells ye. But it
weren't me he hated. I knows dat . . . It wor being
alive wi' all them people living off 'n, putting ye
down, scorning ye fer what ye was. An' the fish gone,
or most of it anyways, and me worrying about money
from one day to the next. Dey was so many of 'em
to look out to. An' it seemed like I was always
reminding him of how he failed us somehow, dough
God knows, I understood, I didn't mean dat. I
wonders now if he understands we at all.

She loads the second wash into the basket.

Lill says the sun'll be out by an' by. P'raps I'll jest
leave 'em till it clears up.

*There are a few clothes left. She puts them in
the tub.*

An' dat waters black now, but it'll have to do fer
what's left.

She starts the washer again and replaces the lid.

At least I got no woollens to worry about today.
Dat nylon's a wonderful t'ing. Washes out like new
everytime. Dey was a time when I 'ad to do the half
o' it be hand. My and dem heavy sweaters Pat used
to wear, stiff wi' all dat old gurry . . .

*She picks up the bowl of washing, takes it to the
porch, puts it down and comes back. She gets a
floor cloth from under the sink and wipes
around the base of the washer.*

The wash don't take no time now, thanks be to God. When I 'ad 'em at home now, eight youngsters and Pat 'an me Mother, God rest their souls, it'd be twice a week, all day, and five lines weighted wi' wash. Dat's some nice sight on a fine day. The clothes dancing, and a smell off 'em like the wind, scented. Coming across all dem old woods, I suppose . . . Picking up the wild blossoms.

She replaces the floor cloth.

All dat silly old stuff dey tells ye on television to put into yer wash now, and to make it smell fresh. Sure, dey's nothing like a summer wind. What could be sweeter dan dat? Though I suppose they doesn't get summer winds, dem dat lives in cities.

She crosses right, plugs in the electric kettle and stands by it waiting.

I wor to Toronto onct. Dat wor when Walter wor stationed at Trenton. My, dey got some lovely shops dere. I could spend all day just walking about dem, looking.

She laughs.

Though where people gits the money from to buy dat stuff, I doesn't know. Be the time I pays fer the grocery each week, an' puts a bit by to git their clothes fer the winter, dey's hardly enough fer the oil. And here I am, needing a new blower fer the stove, and God knows we'll freeze the winter if we don't get 'n and the Welfare says 'tis not their job an' they pays me enough to look after t'ings like that. And where be the Blessed Virgin, am I to git seventy dollars wi' no man working, and two hundred and eighty a month wi' four growing youngsters to school, and the price o' t'ings as dey is?

The kettle has boiled. She takes a mug, puts a teabag into it and carries the tea across to the table where she sits. She lights a cigarette.

'Tis a question of who ye knows, dat's all. Madeline Peak now, up the road, she got her house done top to bottom, new clapboard and new roof and a brand new wood and oil stove, and her sons sending her money from the States, and God knows how much she got salted away, fer ye knows dat old man Peak had money when he died . . . Christ. He nivir paid his sharemen but one half of their wages and dat when he wor bringing home t'ousand o' fish. Dey says she got it in a box under the floorboards in her bedroom. Aye, and the way t'ings is now, it won't be long afore some fellers wi' a few in 'll surprise her some night, her and her box. Olga now, she says dat the welfare officer spent days, aye and nights too, down wi' her afore she got the work done, and she should know, living at the back of 'n. And I allows, he did too, fer no other woman on the island would look at 'n, wi' his watery pigs eyes, an' a nose on him worse than Cracky Hines, poor feller, and him dead these ten years and nivir knowing a maid on account o' it.

She laughs.

I minds Pat now, and Jack and dey, one night afore Christmas, and dey well on wi' the shine, tormenting Cracky something terrible about it. "Dey says a big nose means a big cock," says Pat, sly, winking at the others. Oh, he could be the Divil when he wanted.

She laughs.

And poor old Cracky, grinning and nodding, dat great big nose o' his like a port light winking away. "Dat's right, boy," he says. "Dat's right." And den Jack started 'em singing, and dey all knows dat Cracky couldn't sing to save his life, no, nor wouldn't neither fer he was too shy be half. And it wor sing or show yer piece . . .

She laughs again.

Oh my. And Pat gits a ruler an' says, "Out wi' it, Cracky . . . On the table wid'n . . . What is it now, six?" "Eight at least," says Jack, eyeing Cracky's nose, "eight or ten, I'd say," and Cracky nodding and grinning, fearful embarrassed. "No," cries Pat . . . "Twelve den, we'll try twelve. Come on, out wid 'n," and den Cracky near crying shouts out, "what's de good o' showing it, fer dere's no one would have I anyways." 'Twas a mortal sin to torment him so.

She laughs again.

Dey gives up after dat, an' we nivir did get to see 'n and Cracky nivir got to use 'n, I suppose, and dat's dat. But that Madeline Peak . . . She'd do anything now to git what she wants, and I allows dat's just what she did, fer what other reason could they be fer her to git all dat done, and me with neither blower and hardly a stick o' wood cut and the price o' t'ings scandalous . . . Dey's times, so they is, when I don't know as how I wants to keep on wi' it. P'raps Pat got the best of it after all. He looked happy enough laid out dere in the living room . . . Smile on his face so much as to say . . . "I made it, ye see . . . I got rid of it all now . . . All the torment and worry of it."

She pauses, near tears again.

But I'd give anyt'ing to hear him singing "The Gay Spanish Maid," like he always done when he 'ad a few in, and the boys was all gathered and Jack had the accordian going . . . Didn't seem to matter den dat we got nothing. We was altogether den. An' everyone in the place the same as we, but 'tis as if now we's all separated, like the cream from the milk.

Nobody sings no more. Nobody comes to visit since Pat's been gone. All the youngsters wants is skiddoos and cars and I can't say as 'ow I blame 'em, fer everyone else got one or t' other or both, though God knows hows they pays fer 'em at all. Jack's accordian now, 'asn't bin used dese five years. 'Tis up there in the attic, gatherin' dust. I goes up sometimes, just to look at 'n, to see if it's still dere. An' the dust dat t'ick, I'm afeard to touch the dust . . . 'Tis like all dat's left is memories. If I wor to clean it now, and bring it down, 'twould be no use to no one. It'd be jest an ornament . . . 'Tis better where it be.

The phone rings. It startles her. She jumps up.

My. Dat wash'll be done to death.

She hurriedly crosses to washer, turns it off, and crosses to the phone.

Hello . . . Yis, maid . . .

She pauses.

No . . . I'm about finished. 'Tis stopped, 'as it? No . . . I weren't looking out, maid.

She pauses.

Well, ye knows I'm half afraid to leave the house o' nights, what wi' the youngsters the way dey is. Wild . . .

She pauses.

Yis, girl. Last week when I come home there wor Bernice and Marvin and dat crowd from the bottom, smooching away in the living room wi' the lights off and dat ole record player roaring away . . . I'm like to take dat down to the cove afore the summer's out . . . An the two young ones looking on, maid.

She pauses.

I tells 'em, 'tis not right, such goings on in the house in front o' youngsters, but dey takes no notice o' me, maid, not since Pat's gone. I'm dreading school turning out and dat's a fact . . .

She pauses.

Well, I swears if I took a broom handle to Marvin like I used to do wi' his brother when dey was up to mischief, he'd crack me over the 'ead wi' it. And Bernice . . . Whatever would Pat 'ave made of it at all.

She pauses.

I suppose yer right, maid. Dey get at it whatever we says and dey's a chance of 'em drawing the line in the house, I suppose.

She pauses.

Now ye knows I'd love to go.

She pauses.

Well, I wor just two numbers off the jackpot last week, twelve hundred dollars. My, what couldn't I do wid dat.

She laughs.

Well, I wor sitting dere, maid, waiting, oh, it must've been fer at least ten numbers, waiting fer a rotten ole nine. The sweat wor pouring off me. I 'lows, if they'd called it, I'd have fainted right away.

She laughs.

Tell him to blow at the top den, about eight. Yis, girl, alright. I'll be ready.

She puts down the phone, crosses to the washer and begins to put the last few things through the wringer.

Dat's an awful lot o' money now, twelve hundred dollars. If I wor to win dat, I could tell the old welfare man to stuff his blower up his arse.

She pauses.

Den I could git in to Gander mebbe, and buy the youngsters dere new outfits fer the winter . . . They're growing some fast, I swears I can't keep up wi' 'em at all, and dey isn't content anymore wi' hand me downs . . . They wants nothing but the best, and here's me wi' nothing. It'd be nice dough, if I were to win jest a part o' it. Could git a quarter o' meat and me flour fer the winter an' a deep freeze fer the fish. Dat'd be some nice. And if dere was anyt'ing left den, I could git some nice material fer Lillian to make me a new dress. She makes lovely clothes . . . Her crowd o' girls now always looks as if dey just come from the pages o' a catalogue.

She dreams.

And den I could put some money by to say masses fer Pat and me mother. P'raps Mary Francis could git a nice sung mass fer 'em in the cathedral in St. John's . . . Dat'd be lovely. I minds we used to have 'em as a maid. Dat wor when Father McCarthy wor young and 'ad a choir. He wor an old guilderoy in some ways, but he kept a lovely choir dem days.

She is silent.

But what's the point in dreaming, girl. Ye've nivir won anyt'ing in yer life and I allows, yer not about to. But I'll go to the bingo anyways. 'Tis a bit o' company . . . 'Bout all any o' us gits dese days. Dey says the church takes too much out o' it . . . I doesn't know why folks is surprised . . . Dey've always taken too much to my mind from dem dat can least afford it. I minds Father McCarthy when all of us girls was taking classes fer confirmation . . . "'Tis blessed to be poor," he'd tell us. "Ye'll git yer reward in heaven." Poor old soul. I suppose he wor only trying to help, fer dere's nothing worse dan expecting somet'ing ye ain't going to git, and dat's a fact.

She has been putting the wrung clothes on the washer lid. She now takes them and puts them on top of the others on the porch. She comes back in carrying an empty bucket and begins to empty the washer. She sings . . .

"The gay Spanish maid at the age of sixteen
Through the meadow she roamed far and wide
Beneath the green tree she sat down fer to rest
Wi' her gay gallant youth be her side."

She stops the pump, carries the bucket to the sink and empties the water down it. She comes back and turns to the pump to refill the bucket. She continues to sing . . .

"My ship sails at midnight, my darling, said he,
And with you I may never more roam,
Won't ye meet me tonight when yer parents are at rest,
Won't ye meet me tonight on the shore."

She stops the pump, crosses to sink to empty the bucket and pauses. She hums and pauses again.

I've forgotten most o' dat now. Seems if ye don't keep it up it goes from ye . . .

She frowns and hums. She recollects a verse. She bends down to get the floor cloth from beneath the sink and goes back to the washer to wipe the tub.

105

"The moon which had risen shone over the deep,
The water and sky seemed to meet
But the only sad sound was the murmuring waves
As they broke on the rock at her feet."

*When she has finished wiping the tub, she puts
the lid on. She pushes it back towards the sink
and dries her hands on a hand towel.*

Ye knows, dat's something I've taken to doing meself
lately . . . Expecting something fer nothing. 'Tis
sometimes I've nivir done before, but seems like the
whole place be going round wid dere hands out, an'
'tis catching. But what can ye do? 'Tis not as if I
didn't work, God knows . . . I've nivir known a day
when I didn't work and I suppose now I must wait
fer me old age pension as a sign from someone dat
I've done well. And if I lives long enough to git it,
I 'lows I'll not live long enough to enjoy it. Dere's
Miss Milly now, hanging on fer grim deat' till she's
a hundred so's she kin git a telegram from the
Queen. Yis, an I suppose the Queen lives to be a
hundred she'll expect telegrams from all o' us. Well,
she can kiss me arse. 'Tis an awful t'ing fer a woman
on her own when all she do be waiting fer is the
governmint to pay her fer living sixty-five years . . .
I tells Miss Milly she's foolish, but what kin ye
expect when yer middle name's Victoria . . .

*She unplugs the washer, folds up the cord and
puts it inside. She crosses the room to pick up
the detergent and bleach and puts them back
inside the washer.*

But den, dey had it different from us. Dey nivir asked
no questions of no one. If dere men died, 'twas the
will o' God. If dey was no fish, 'twas the will o'
God. If dere youngsters was taken sick, and dey
was no doctor this fifty mile and much o' that across
water, they'd wait for 'n to die and dat was the will
o' God. Pat . . . He wor a good Catholic in some

106

ways . . . drove us all to mass on Sunday, but I wondered times whether he done it 'cos he always done it, and his father afore him, and it give him a link wi' somet'ing. I'm half inclined to t'ink he didn't believe in the will o' God though. T'ings 'ad 'appened to make him angry. Like de time Joe Green an' his brother went trew the ice an' dey having no business on it all, fer the wind 'ad come up western, and she wor breaking up, and dey wid a few in, but dey was wild, dem two, an' wild fer the taste o' seal meat. It wor Pat went out wi' Jack when it come on dark to look for 'n. I didn't want 'n to go, fer the sea wor some fierce outside, but he told me to mind me own business. As if he weren't me business, nor Jack neither, me first born. "Dey's kin," he said. "And if dey weren't, i'd go anyways." An' I sitting wi' the rosary fer t'ree hours, God help me, fer when it's times like dat, ye've nowhere else to run. First off he tole me, dey t'ought dey'd hit a deadhead in the water . . . some t'ree miles out or so, following a lead t'rough the pack. And it breaking up and growlers turning over, and it dark and dey taking water so dat Jack wor all the time bailing to keep her up. But it weren't no piece o' timber. It wor Joe. Frozen solid, he wor . . . couple o' feet below the water. They cast about fer a spell den looking for t' other one, but wor like to be lost demselves, so Pat come on back wi' him. Dey nivir did find his brother . . . Took eighteen hours to thaw'n out so dey could arrange him in his coffin . . . And his eyes gone in the time he wor in the water. Pat nivir said a word all night. Sat up an' got drunk den fell asleep be the stove an' Jack wor dat wore out, he fell asleep on the day bed, oilskins and all. He wor but fifteen den. Den Father McCarthy at the wake says as how we was all brothers o' the sea and must trust to God in His Wisdom to hold us, or let us fall when he wanted 'n. Pat went redder 'n a pot of jam. "God 'adn't not'ing to do wi' it, Father," he says, very quiet. Ye could 'ave 'eard a pin drop fer dey was all dere . . . Mary and dey, and the fambly. "It was dem," he said,

" and the way it is here, an' who knows but dey didn't want to go dat way, fer there's damn all to keep us." An' dey was just Mary sobbing quiet, no other sound, and poor Joe in his coffin wi' his eyes bandaged dat folks mightn't be too stricken. He left den. I minds Father McCarthy's face, as white as Pat's wor red. But he said nar' word about it. Not den. Not ever. I wondered den if Pat wor half expecting to drown hisself dat night, 'ad jest gone out not caring, though nivir another man in the cove would've launched his boat in dat gale o' wind. 'Tis funny. Ye lives wi' a person all yer life, and ye nivir knows 'n. An' if dat's true, what's the point of it at all? Is we all to be strangers? 'Tis too cruel to be borned jest fer dat.

She crosses to the table and lights a cigarette.

Funny, how I talks to meself now, and yit all the time Pat wor alive, we nivir talked o' things like dat. We was both too shy, I 'llows . . . Dere's youngsters to take yer mind of t'ings, an' the talk o' the days work, men's work mostly, and the worry o' making ends meet, and a bit o' gossip, and when the winter come, the drinking, and the singing, an' the fool tricks we played on each other, like dat time wi' Cracky Hines. I suppose it wor best to leave t'ings be. Oh my.

She gets up, stacks the dishes and takes them across to the sink where she dumps them in.

If the weather holds, I must git the boys to turn the garden and put me potatoes in. Though 'tis a torment trying to git 'em to do anyt'ing. If I kin git t'ree sacks the year, it'll be a godsend. I wonders, should I let Morgan go fishing wi' Marvin when schools out? He's awful young, but Marvin's a good boy on the water, jest like his brother was. Pat taught 'em well, and dey's no fear in dem at all, though dey's times a bit o' it might stand 'em in good stead. P'raps dey could git enough den to keep theirselves in money the summer, and buy a few clothes maybe. 'Twould be a help. If dey does well, I might take Marvin out o' school next year and den he kin go to night school. Dey pays 'em for doing dat, Lill says. I doesn't know though. He's doing well at his books and God knows, I shouldn't be the one to hold 'n back, though 'twould be good to have 'n about the house fer a year or two yit to help wi' t'ings. I'm sure I doesn't know what to do wi' Bernice . . . She'll nivir make Grade 11 the way she carries on. I'm afeard fer her. Time was when ye could git a daughter into service in a nice home, but now dat's not good enough fer 'em. Dey wants to be secretaries and hairdressers and I don't know what. Oh well, I suppose she'll git somet'ing by an' by, if she stays out o' trouble.

> *She pushes back the washer until it's parallel to the sink.*

Some expensive, girls. If I 'ad me time back, I'd 'ave had all boys. Dey's a torment but dey ain't half as much trouble when dey gits to their teens. Still and all, she helps about the house, and I suppose I kin git her to come berry picking wi' me in the fall. Lill says the price be going up dis year . . . An so it should . . . A dollar a gallon I got last year, and me out from dawn to dusk on me knees picking, picking until I couldn't see no more, the sun on the berries blinding ye. I swears dat's what's wrong wi' me eyes now. Dat old sun on the berries. But 'tis some nice on a good day when ye stops fer lunch, the kittle going on a few sticks, and ye looking down over the hill at the water, the men at the hand lines den, and the spire o' the old church on Duck Island sticking up whiter 'n whalebone. I minds dat time . . . the year afore Pat died, when dey had mass out dere. All the families going off in the boats, sun beating the water till it shone like dat old copper pan me mother 'ad till the feller come from Toronto and give her a couple o' dollars fer it. I minds it well . . . All the

109

boats stretched out across the ocean fer seven miles, and den anchoring in the cove, and all of us saying hello, and smiling like we were met fer the first time. An' the church wor full, and we all spilled out on the grass, and the gulls and the murrs and the tansies and the puffins setting up the great din and all around the ocean . . . nothing but ocean . . . shining in the sun. Dey says the church be two hundred year old . . . I don't know about dat . . . But the winders are some old fashioned. Dey was right low, ye could see right t'rough the aisle, and from the inside all ye could see about ye was ocean still . . . And dere we all was, and the priest 'ad brought loudspeakers wired to some kind o' battery, an' we said mass out dere, on Duck Island, in the sun, kneeling on the grass. Pat knelt next to me, and Walter and Marvin and Mary Francis . . . She wor home den, and Morgan and Bernice . . . "I believe in God the Father Almighty, Creator o' Heaven and Earth and in Jesus Christ, His only begotten Son." I minds the Creed. An' I looked across at Pat and he wor crying. I nivir durst say anyt'ing to 'n. Nivir mentioned it.

She pauses.

And after the mass, we all had a picnic, an' the fires was going an' the beer flowing . . . Well, don't say we nivir had the good time. It seemed den it wor the beginning o' something, but I t'inks now, it wor the other way about. It wor the end of it, somehow. We nivir done it agin. And when I gits to the island dese days, once or twice a summer, it makes me sad to t'ink on it. Seemed like we was at the top o' some kind of curve and from den on, it wor all down hill. Pat, he knew. An' I suppose it's only jest coming to me. And I'm not sure whether I wants to know about it or not. I should jest git on, I suppose, fer a few more years and not mind nothing, till dey've gone. Till dey've all left me. I minds how Pat, the week afore he died, it wor . . . I minds how he said . . . It'd come on to snow something fierce . . . "It'd be nice, maid," he said, "if when dey's all gone, when all the young-sters on the whole bloody island has upped and gone, if dey was a nice old people's home fer us to crawl into until we dies. Think on it," he said. "someone fer to wait on ye a bit, git yer meals, wake ye in the morning and tell ye when to git to bed o' nights. Don't ye t'ink dat'd be nice, maid?" An' I said, "I don't know, Pat, boy, I doesn't know at all."

She begins to cry and wipes her tears with her apron.

And dey goes and does it now, dere be no point in me going on me own boy, would dere?

She struggles to control herself, then goes down-stage and looks out.

Well, damn dat. 'Tis raining agin. An' I suppose it rains forever dis wash is goin' out. Come on, Therese, girl. Come on. Dey's no point in grieving . . . None at all. 'Twas long enough ago ye made yer bed, and I 'llows, ye've some time left to lie on it . . .

She crosses to the porch, picks up the bowl of clothes and exits.

TALONBOOKS — PLAYS IN PRINT 1976

Colours in the Dark — James Reaney
The Ecstasy of Rita Joe — George Ryga
Captives of the Faceless Drummer — George Ryga
Crabdance — Beverley Simons
Listen to the Wind — James Reaney
Ashes for Easter & Other Monodramas — David Watmough
Esker Mike & His Wife, Agiluk — Herschel Hardin
Sunrise on Sarah — George Ryga
Walsh — Sharon Pollock
Apple Butter & Other Plays for Children — James Reaney
The Factory Lab Anthology — Connie Brissenden, ed.
The Trial of Jean-Baptiste M. — Robert Gurik
Battering Ram — David Freeman
Hosanna — Michel Tremblay
Les Belles Soeurs — Michel Tremblay
API 2967 — Robert Gurik
You're Gonna Be Alright Jamie Boy — David Freeman
Bethune — Rod Langley
Preparing — Beverley Simons
Forever Yours Marie-Lou — Michel Tremblay
En Pièces Détachées — Michel Tremblay
Lulu Street — Ann Henry
Three Plays by Eric Nicol — Eric Nicol
Fifteen Miles of Broken Glass — Tom Hendry
Bonjour, là, Bonjour — Michel Tremblay
Jacob's Wake — Michael Cook
On the Job — David Fennario
Sqrieux-de-Dieu — Betty Lambert
Some Angry Summer Songs — John Herbert
The Execution — Marie-Claire Blais
Tiln & Other Plays — Michael Cook
Great Wave of Civilization — Herschel Hardin
La Duchesse de Langeais & Other Plays — Michel Tremblay
Have — Julius Hay